MONOGRAPHS OF THE
SOCIETY FOR RESEARCH IN
CHILD DEVELOPMENT

SERIAL NO. 217, VOL. 53, NO. 1

PEER INTERACTION
OF YOUNG CHILDREN

CAROLLEE HOWES

UNIVERSITY OF CALIFORNIA, LOS ANGELES

WITH COMMENTARY BY
KENNETH H. RUBIN AND HILDY S. ROSS
DORAN C. FRENCH

MONOGRAPHS OF THE SOCIETY FOR RESEARCH IN CHILD
DEVELOPMENT, SERIAL NO. 217, VOL. 53, NO. 1

CONTENTS

ABSTRACT

HOWES, CAROLLEE. Peer Interaction of Young Children. With Commentary
by KENNETH H. RUBIN and HILDY S. ROSS and DORAN C. FRENCH. *Monographs of the Society for Research in Child Development*, 1987, **53**(1, Serial
No. 217).

Classroom observations and teacher and sociometric ratings described
peer interactions and friendships of 1–6-year-old children enrolled in full-
time child care. The study was both cross-sectional ($N = 329$) and longitudinal in design. 41 children were followed for 3 years and 223 children for 2
years.

The purpose of the study was to assess predicted sequences and individual differences in the early development of social competence with peers.
The study results supported these predictions. Complementary and reciprocal social play emerged when the children were 1 year old, and social
pretend play emerged at age 2. Clusters of behavior hypothesized to index
early social competence at each of the age periods studied were validated.

Relations between preschool social classifications of children (sociometric status, social participation, and mutual friendships) were consistent
with earlier research on social status and social withdrawal from peers. Children classified as rejected were rebuffed by their peers when they attempted
play group entry, and children classified as withdrawn were less socially
mature. Children classified as rejected but who had reciprocated friendships
had easier entries into play groups than children classified as rejected with
no reciprocated friendships.

Children's experiences with peers in general and their experiences
within stable peer groups were related to individual differences in social
competence with peers. Experiences with peers but not with siblings were
associated with increased social competence with peers.

Children's dyadic friendship relationships tended to be maintained.
Children who stayed in the peer group but lost a large proportion of their
friends because their friends moved away showed declines in their frequency of competent social behavior with peers during the subsequent year.

I. INTRODUCTION

All children face the tasks of making friends and getting along with other children. They experience the intimacy and the conflict inherent in human relationships through interactions with peers and learn important social skills within the peer culture. Children learn to lead and to follow others, to collaborate on problem solving, and to cooperate in play.

Some children find peer relationships easy. They have many friends and are considered socially competent by their teachers. Others experience difficulty establishing and maintaining friendships. Their contacts with peers may be hostile or unpleasant. They may withdraw from peer contact, or their peers may reject them. These socially incompetent children are at risk for poor social adjustment in later life (Hartup, 1983).

As a consequence of changes in women's work and the perception of child care, many children begin daily intimate contact with peers during infancy. In this research, I studied the development of social competence with peers in children who had early and sustained peer contacts.

The study tested the assumptions that children's development of social competence with peers precedes in an orderly, sequential fashion and that early individual differences predict later social competence. In subsequent sections, I will define social competence with peers and propose developmental sequences for two aspects of social competence with peers: social interaction and friendship formation. Within each of these aspects of competence and in three different age periods, I identify a behavioral construct to represent developmentally appropriate individual differences. These constructs are used to predict individual differences in competence within and across age periods. Finally, I examine relations between variations in social experiences and social competence with peers.

I define social competence with peers as behavior that reflects successful social functioning with peers (Howes, 1987). Since peer relationships are dyadic and reciprocal, success in social functioning with peers implies that the child is popular and effective in her effect on peers and that the child is sensitive to social communications from peers. This definition of social com-

1

petence includes two independent yet related aspects: social interaction skills and friendships. Social interaction skills include ease of entry into play groups, play with peers, affective expressions, and other behaviors that lead to peer acceptance and popularity (Dodge, 1983; Hartup, 1983). Friendships are defined as stable, dyadic relationships marked by reciprocity and shared positive affect (Howes, 1983). Children who are friends seek each other out, prefer to be together, and enjoy each other's company.

Social interaction skills and friendship may not appear to be independent. Children who are competent in social interaction usually have friends, and children who have friends are often competent in social interaction. Some children, however, have friends but are not generally popular or skillful in social interaction (Masters & Furman, 1981). Furthermore, children engage in qualitatively different social interaction with friends than with acquaintances (Doyle, Connolly, & Rivest, 1980; Gottman, 1983; Roopnarine & Field, 1984).

Sequences in cognitive development underlie early social competence with peers. Social interaction skills with peers are limited by cognitive capacities (Brownell, 1986; Howes, 1985, 1987). For example, children do not engage in social pretend play with peers before they acquire the symbolic function. Social interaction skills with peers should emerge in a sequential fashion on the basis of underlying cognitive changes. Using descriptive literature and pilot observations, I identified behavioral constructs representing social competence with peers within three different age periods and across the domains of social interaction and friendship. I selected age periods that correspond to qualitative changes in cognitive development (Howes, 1987). This sequence is presented visually in Table 1 and is elaborated in subsequent sections of this chapter.

SOCIAL INTERACTION

Sequences in Social Interaction Competence with Peers

The behavioral constructs representing competent social interaction with peers are, as seen in Table 1, complementary and reciprocal play, communication of meaning, and social knowledge of the peer group. These behavioral constructs are expected to emerge in children's peer play in sequential fashion between the toddler and the preschool age periods.

Early toddler period.—I hypothesized that the construct that represents competence in social interaction between the ages of 13 and 24 months (the early toddler period) is the ability to engage in complementary and reciprocal social interaction (see Table 1). Complementary and reciprocal social interaction is the ability to exchange turns and roles in action (Mueller &

TABLE 1

Constructs Representing Social Competence with Peers

Age Period	Social Interaction	Friendship Formative
Early toddler (13–24 months)	Complementary and reciprocal play	Stable friendships
Late toddler (25–36 months)	Communication of meaning	Flexibility of friendships
Preschool (3–5 years)	Social knowledge of the peer group	Differentiation of friends from playmates

Lucas, 1975). Children engage in different but complementary activities, such as run and chase, hide and seek, offer and receive. The interaction structure of complementary and reciprocal play is analogous to social play as defined by Eckerman and Stein (1982), game structures as defined by Goldman and Ross (1978) and Ross (1982), and complementary behavioral roles as defined by Brownell (1986).

Mueller (Mueller & Lucas, 1975) suggests that complementary and reciprocal play represents the ability to assume the role of the other in action. Cognitive and linguistic capacities associated with the emergence of complementary and reciprocal play include the sequencing of words into sentences, the sequencing of pretend acts into scripts, and decentration (Brownell, 1986; Howes, 1987).

Late toddler period.—The communication of meaning (see Table 1), defined as the joint understanding of the theme of the interaction (Brenner & Mueller, 1982; Howes, 1985, 1987), represents social competence between 25 and 36 months (the late toddler period). I studied the communication of meaning in the context of social pretend play. Children must sustain complementary and reciprocal interaction while sharing the nonliteral themes of the play in order to engage in social pretend play (Howes, 1985). In cooperative social pretend play, the most advanced social pretend play examined in the current study, children assume complementary pretend roles while engaging in interactive social play. Cooperative social pretend play emerges during the late toddler period and is dependent on the acquisition of the symbolic function (Howes, 1985, 1987).

Complementary and reciprocal peer play is expected to precede cooperative social pretend play (see Table 1). The two forms of play are structurally similar. In both forms, the different but complementary role of the partner is acknowledged, and the action of the partner is reversed. In complementary and reciprocal peer play action, roles (e.g., chased and chaser) are reversed. In cooperative social pretend play, pretend roles (e.g., bus driver and passenger) are reversed (Garvey, 1977; Howes, 1985; Rubin, Fein, & Vandenberg, 1983). Cooperative social pretend play requires the communication of meaning to achieve role reversal. Children must understand that their partner is acting out a role. In complementary and reciprocal play, the children do not communicate the meaning of their actions. I assumed that children who are acquiring cooperative social pretend play can build on the reversal structure already established in complementary and reciprocal peer play by adding newly acquired nonliteral, symbolic content to existing play structures. Therefore, complementary and reciprocal play was expected to emerge before cooperative social pretend play.

Preschool period.—I expected that children's social knowledge of the peer group would follow the development of their ability to communicate meaning (see Table 1). Once children are able to use symbolic behaviors in peer interaction, their range of potential playmates dramatically increases. Children who can communicate meaning in social interaction are no longer dependent on routines and idiosyncratic communication patterns they developed with familiar peers. They can name a game (e.g., "ride bikes") or specify the design of the play by saying, "You're the mommy and I'm the baby." Therefore, preschoolers tend to play with a wider range of playmates than do toddlers (Howes, 1983; Lederberg, Rosenblatt, Vandell, & Chapin, 1987). When children play with many different peers, they acquire knowledge of the different play styles and characteristic behaviors of their peers.

Sociometric interviews that assess individual differences in social competence with peers in preschool children (Asher, Singleton, Tinsley, & Hymel, 1979; Hartup, 1983; Hymel, 1983) are based on their social knowledge of the peer group (see Table 1). In order to complete a sociometric interview reliably, a child must be aware of group membership, have knowledge of behavioral characteristics of individuals within the group, and have the ability to make stable personal judgments about these behavioral characteristics.

Children's social knowledge of the peer group was not directly assessed in the current study. I indirectly assessed social knowledge of the peer group by using sociometric techniques as one measure of individual differences in preschool social competence with peers.

In summary, I have hypothesized a sequence of behavioral constructs representing development in social interaction competence with peers. I expected children to engage in complementary and reciprocal social play at earlier ages than they engage in cooperative social pretend play.

Individual Differences within Developmental Periods

All children are presumed to develop social competence with peers in the sequence outlined in Table 1. I did not study whether a child engages in the behavioral construct and individual differences in mastering the se-

quence. Instead, I expected individual differences between children to occur in the relative proportion of the time the child engages in the behavioral
cluster representing social competence for the age period. Differences in the
relative proportion of complementary play with peers represent individual
differences in the early toddler period, differences in the relative proportion of cooperative social pretend play represent individual differences in
the late toddler period, and differences in sociometric status represent individual differences in the preschool period. Individual differences in sociometric status are associated with concurrent social competence in preschool and older children (Coie & Dodge, 1983; Coie & Kupersmidt, 1983;
Dodge, 1983; Dodge, Schlundt, Schocken, & Delugach, 1983; Hartup,
1983; Ladd, 1983; Rubin & Daniels-Beirness, 1983).

I used alternative measures of social competence with peers—ease of
entry into play groups and teacher ratings—to validate individual differences within periods. Entry behaviors are associated with sociometric status
in preschool and school age children (Dodge, 1983; Dodge et al., 1983;
Putallaz, 1983; Putallaz & Gottman, 1981). Teachers experience the child in
a variety of interactions that may not be captured using observational measures. Teacher ratings also are efficient, economical, reliable, and valid assessments of social competence (Baumrind, 1968; Greenwood, Walker,
Todd, & Hops, 1979; LaFreniere & Sroufe, 1985; Rubin & Clark, 1983;
Sroufe, 1983).

Stability of Individual Differences in Social Competence with Peers across Developmental Periods

I expected individual differences in social competence with peers to
remain stable across developmental periods (Howes, 1987). In contrast, I
expected relative frequencies of observed behaviors to be only moderately
stable over the entire age range because qualitative as well as quantitative
changes occur across developmental periods in the mode of interaction with
peers. Children who engaged in a high proportion of complementary and
reciprocal peer play in the early toddler period were expected to engage in a
high proportion of cooperative social pretend play in the late toddler period
and to receive high ratings from peers and teachers in the preschool period.

The structural similarities between complementary and reciprocal peer
play and cooperative social pretend play (Garvey, 1977; Howes, 1985; Rubin
et al., 1983) suggest that children who are competent in social play in the
early toddler period also will be competent in social pretend play in the late
toddler period. Individual differences in both forms of play may represent
an underlying competence in social-emotional development that would be
expected to remain stable (Bronson, 1981, 1985).

Participation in social pretend play requires a flexible repertoire of social behaviors, socially relevant cognitive skills, and the willingness to cooperate, to share, and to compromise in the definition of the play (Rubin et al., 1983). The skills required for social pretend play are similar to those associated with sociometric status (Coie & Kupersmidt, 1983; Dodge, 1983; Dodge et al., 1983; Hartup, 1983; Ladd, 1983; Rubin & Daniels-Beirness, 1983). Therefore, I expected individual differences in cooperative social pretend play to be associated with later individual differences in sociometric status. Connolly and Doyle (1984) and Rosenberg (1985) report concurrent relations between preschoolers' participation in social pretend play and a number of measures of social competence, including sociometric status.

Sociometric ratings assessed individual differences in preschool social competence. Individual differences in sociometric status remain relatively stable from kindergarten to grade 1 (Rubin & Daniels-Beirness, 1983) and within middle childhood (Coie & Dodge, 1983). Kindergarten sociometric status is predictive of teacher ratings of social adjustment 3 years later (Li, 1985). There are no data, however, on the degree to which preschool sociometric status predicts later social competence. Therefore, I also tested the predictive sequence using teacher ratings as a measure of preschool social competence.

FRIENDSHIPS

The behavioral constructs outlined in Table 1 for friendships represent qualitative changes between the toddler and the preschool periods. As with the behavioral constructs for social interaction skills, these constructs emerge in a predictable sequence and represent individual differences in social competence within age period. In this work, friendships are reciprocal. Reciprocal friendships are defined by mutual attraction and liking. Both children select the other as a friend.

Early toddler period.—The early toddler period is marked by stable friendships (see Table 1). Children in the early toddler period differentiate among their available playmates. They direct a disproportionate amount of their social overtures, social responses, and mutual positive affect to one or two children within the group (Howes, 1983; Vandell & Mueller, 1980). In a short-term longitudinal study, Howes (1983) found these earliest friendships to be stable over a school year. In the current study, I examined the stability of friendships over a 3-year period.

Toddler friendships are marked by emotional responsiveness (Howes, 1983). Two studies suggest that stable toddler friendships may be a form of emotional attachment. Freud and Dann (1951) report that toddler age peers can serve as attachment figures under extreme circumstances of maternal deprivation. Small (1976) also reports that toddler friends can reduce distress in the absence of the mother. Because toddler friendships have this affective quality, I expected some friendships formed in the toddler period to remain stable through the preschool period.

Late toddler period.—I expected children in the late toddler period to have more friends than younger children because friendships become more flexible (see Table 1). They also were expected to differentiate between the functions of different friendships, such as friends for playing running games versus friends to use in times of emotional stress (Howes, 1987). Flexibility of friendships is the construct representing late toddler friendships because children increasingly use symbols in their play with peers. For example, children's ability to use language in their games makes them more flexible in their choice of a partner. Presymbolic children must rely on rituals and routines to communicate with peers, while children with the symbolic function can communicate with commonly understood symbols (talk, signs, and pretend games).

As children's friendships increase in flexibility, identifying friendships becomes more difficult. During the early toddler period, when children have only a few stable friendships and play with only a few peers, high agreement is reported between behavioral and teacher identifications of friendships (Howes, 1983). As children increasingly differentiate between the emotional and play components of friendships, and as they play with a larger range of peers, the behavioral identification of friendships becomes more difficult (Hinde, Titmus, Easton, & Tamplin, 1985). In the current study, I used three methods of identification of friendships—behavioral identification based on earlier work by Howes (1983), teacher nominations, and reciprocated sociometric nominations.

Preschool period.—In the preschool period, children begin to differentiate friends from playmates (see Table 1). Preschool friends, as compared to playmates, exchange more positive and less negative behaviors (Masters & Furman, 1981), show more reciprocity (Foot, Chapman, & Smith, 1980; Lederberg et al., 1987), and are more responsive (Howes, 1983). Social cognitive studies of friendship (e.g., Furman & Bierman, 1983) suggest that, with age, children differentiate playmates from intimate associates. I examined the differentiation of friendships from playmates during the preschool period in several different ways. I examined relations between friendships and success at group entry, differences between children who did and did not have reciprocal friends, and relations between reciprocal friendship and social status. I also examined the function of stable friendships for social competence with peers.

Preschoolers play with children they do not consider friends (Tessier & Boivin, 1985). The range of nonfriend children with whom the child will play may be restricted. Children use temporary friendship status as a means of obtaining play group entry (e.g., "I'll be your friend if I can play," or,

"You're my friend, Right?" Corsaro, 1981). Children may permit entry and assign temporary friendship status only to those children they generally like. Children who are sociometrically rejected by peers may be refused entry and denied temporary friendship status. I examined this hypothesis by comparing the success of attempts to enter peer groups of children of different social status. I expected children who were rejected by peers to be less successful in entering groups. I also expected rejected children who had reciprocated friendships to be more successful at entry if their friend was a group member.

There is no one-to-one correspondence between sociometric status and friendship patterns. While it is unlikely that a child classified as popular would have no reciprocal friendships, the reverse is not true. A child who is neglected or rejected by the peer group as a whole still may have reciprocated friendships (Masters & Furman, 1981). Elsewhere (Howes, 1983), I have suggested that younger children develop social skills within the context of stable friendship relationships. The child with reciprocated friendships may develop competent social interaction with peers regardless of sociometric status. I examined this notion by comparing the social interactive competence of neglected and rejected children with and without friends.

I expected to find some preschool children in the current study who had no reciprocated friendships. Interaction with friends is more intimate, often including self-disclosure and fantasy play, than is interaction with acquaintances or unfamiliar partners (Doyle et al., 1980; Gottman, 1983; Roopnarine & Field, 1984). Children who do not have friends tend to watch their peers, while those with friends engage in multifaceted interaction (Roopnarine & Field, 1984). Therefore, in the current study, I expected to find children without friendships to be less socially competent in social interaction with peers.

Finally, preschool children form both stable and temporary friendships (Howes, 1983; Lederberg et al., 1987). Play behaviors observed in the two types of friendships are different (Howes, 1983; Lederberg et al., 1987). Stable friends play in a more complex and responsive manner than temporary friends. Stable friendships serve the affective needs of the child. Temporary friendships, in contrast, center on shared interests and activities. In the current study, stable friendships were defined as friendships that were maintained for at least a year. I examined the proportion of young children's friendships that were highly stable and the association between friendship stability and social competence with peers.

I also investigated the emotional significance of early friendship relationships by examining separations from friends. One consequence of early experience with peers is that a child almost inevitably experiences the loss of a friend. Most children in the sample experienced this loss either by moving to a new child care center and to a new peer group or by losing a reciprocal friend because the friend changed child care arrangements. Hartup (1975) has called for descriptive data on the incidence and the persistence of children's responses to separation from peers. Separation distress suggests that friendships between young peers may have some of the affective qualities of adult friendships. Field (1984) has documented short-term distress in child care children after the separation from friends and acquainted peers. She found changes in patterns of affect and behavior and in physiological measures of stress immediately following separation. I designed the current study to assess more long-term effects of separation. I explored changes in the play behaviors of children who remained in their peer groups 9 months after their friends moved away.

VARIATIONS IN SOCIAL EXPERIENCES

Children in our society vary widely in their social experiences with peers. Some children enter peer groups as infants and remain with the same group of children until they begin kindergarten. Others begin peer experiences as infants but move between several different groups of children as they change child care arrangements. Still others are home with their mothers and perhaps siblings until joining a same-age peer group as a toddler or preschooler.

I expected these variations in children's experiences with peers would be associated with individual differences in their social competence with peers. The complexity of early peer interaction is more strongly associated with peer experience than with age (Howes, 1980; Mueller & Brenner, 1977), but little research has been done with older children.

Individual differences in social competence with peers in children with more and less peer experience may be due to differences between adults and peers as social partners. Peers are less responsive and sensitive to children's communication attempts than adults (Hay, 1985). Peers also have different interests than do adults (Rubenstein & Howes, 1976). For example, few peers are willing to listen to a 2-year-old's rendition of a song, but they are very happy to jump off a step 20 times in a row. Therefore, engaging in play with peers may require particular social abilities that are best acquired in the peer context and are less likely to be acquired in adult-child interaction.

It is important to distinguish between experiences with peers in general and experiences with particular peers. A child might have 2 years of full-time daily contact with peers and thus have general experience with peers. If, however, this child was in six different peer groups over the 2-year period, she would have limited experience with any particular peer. Experience with particular peers as well as experience with peers in general facilitates social competence in infants and toddlers (Howes, 1983; Mueller & Brenner, 1977). Experiences with particular peers within a highly stable peer group may contribute to building familiar routines and thus to an increased proportion of complex play behaviors (Howes, 1983). Within peer groups of older children, however, experience with specific peers may have negative consequences because children's social reputations solidify (Coie & Kupersmidt, 1983). Peers may be so influenced by a child's reputation that they fail to perceive changes in the child's social behaviors. For example, Coie and Kupersmidt (1983) report that children classified as neglected within stable peer groups were not necessarily classified as neglected in newly formed groups. In the current study, I examined associations between social competence with peers and children's experiences with peers.

SUMMARY

This chapter has described a set of hypotheses regarding the sequence of development of social competence with peers. These hypotheses are based on three assumptions. (1) The specified sequence of behavioral constructs remains constant across children with variations in their experiences with peers and social relationships with adults. (2) Variations in the behavioral construct used to represent social competence within each developmental period correspond to variations in the social competence of the children. (3) Individual differences in social competence remain stable across developmental periods. Although there are several sources of individual differences in children's social competence with peers (e.g., children's attachments to care givers, Sroufe, 1983), only one potential source, children's experiences with peers, is examined in the current study. Subsequent chapters will elaborate the testing of the hypotheses.

II. DEFINITION AND
MEASUREMENT OF CONSTRUCTS

SAMPLE

Overview of Sample Recruitment

The sample was selected by including all the children in three child care centers that served infants and toddlers. The children in these centers were enrolled in the study in the spring of year 1. Between years 1 and 2 of the study, many of the children changed child care centers. By the spring of year 2, they were enrolled in seven different centers, including the original three. All the children in the four new child care centers were recruited into the study. In order to increase the sample size further, 15 classrooms of children from child care centers serving preschoolers were also recruited in year 2. By the spring of year 3, the year 1 children were attending nine different centers. The year 3 sample includes children enrolled in one of these nine child care centers and the children from the two largest of the child care centers sampled in year 2. Three overlapped samples were thus formed: a cross-sectional sample and two longitudinal samples.

Cross-sectional Sample

A total of 329 children between 12 and 53 months of age participated in the cross-sectional sample. Cross-sectional data were collected in year 2 of the 3-year period of data collection. Demographic and peer experience information for the cross-sectional sample are presented in Table 2. "Months in peer group" refers to the time children had been enrolled in the peer group in which they were observed. "Age entered daily peer experience" refers to the age in months at which children were enrolled in a child care center or family day care home in which there was at least one other child within 1 year of their age. "Group size" refers to the number of chil-

TABLE 2

CROSS-SECTIONAL SAMPLE CHARACTERISTICS

	AGE IN YEARS					
	1	2	3	4	5	6
Number	34	43	56	78	75	43
Sex:						
Girls	14	22	28	39	38	23
Boys	20	21	29	39	36	20
Sibling status:						
Oldest	0	2	13	31	30	10
Youngest	7	11	16	22	27	18
Only	27	30	27	25	18	15
Months in peer						
group (range) ..	10.1	13.2	16.5	11.6	13.8	17.3
	(6–18)	(8–30)	(8–43)	(8–46)	(8–60)	(10–30)
Age entered						
daily peer						
experience						
(range)	8.1	12.8	15.8	35.5	37.2	52.9
	(2–17)	(2–28)	(2–37)	(2–50)	(2–51)	(2–57)
Family structure:						
Two parent	22	35	45	59	60	30
Single parent	12	8	11	19	15	13
Mean group size	10	18	24	24	25	25
Mean adult to						
child ratio	1:4	1:5	1:10	1:12	1:12	1:12

dren within a self-contained unit in the child care center. "Adult to child ratio" refers to the number of children cared for by each adult.

Fifty percent of the children in the cross-sectional sample were Anglo in ethnic background, 20% Asian, 20% black, and 10% Hispanic. All the children came from working-class or professional families.

All children were enrolled in child care full time while their parents worked or attended school. The child care centers were open from approximately 7:00 A.M. to 6:00 P.M., and children typically spent 8 hours per day in the center. No child attended for less than 6 hours per day.

Longitudinal Samples

Demographic and peer experience information for the two longitudinal samples is presented in Table 3. Longitudinal sample 1 consists of children recruited in study year 1. In year 1, they ranged in age from 16 to 33 months. These children were observed each year of the study.

Longitudinal sample 2 was made up of children recruited in year 2. They were observed in year 3 if they remained in the same child care center or, as in the case of 20 children, moved to another child care center in which

TABLE 3

LONGITUDINAL SAMPLES' CHARACTERISTICS

A. LONGITUDINAL SAMPLE 1

	OBSERVATIONS		
	1 (N = 43)	2 (N = 42)	3 (N = 41)
Age range (months)	16–33	28–45	40–57
Sex:			
Girls	22	21	21
Boys	21	21	20
Family structure:			
Two parent	35	34	33
Single parent	8	8	8
Stability of peer group:			
Remained in group	...	19	21
Moved with peers	...	18	7
Moved alone	...	5	13

B. LONGITUDINAL SAMPLE 2

	AGE IN YEARS WHEN FIRST OBSERVED				
	1 (N = 34)	2 (N = 36)	3 (N = 35)	4 (N = 60)	5 (N = 58)
Sex:					
Girls	17	19	18	29	30
Boys	17	17	17	31	28
Family structure:					
Two parent	22	28	28	44	44
Single parent	12	8	7	16	14
Stability of peer group:					
Remained in group	32	25	18	15	7
Changed within school	0	7	3	45	51
Moved with peers	0	2	7	0	0
Moved alone	2	2	7	0	0

observations were being carried out in year 3. Longitudinal sample 2 represents a somewhat more stable population than longitudinal sample 1 because I did not track the majority of these children when they changed centers. Longitudinal sample 2, therefore, is primarily composed of children who remained in stable peer groups. There were no ethnic or social class differences between the samples of children. There were also no differences in the amount of time each day the children spent in child care.

Children from longitudinal sample 1 ($N = 41$) appear in the cross-sectional sample only in their second year of data collection. Children from longitudinal sample 2 ($N = 223$) appear in the cross-sectional sample only in their first year of data collection.

MEASURES AND PROCEDURES

Observations

Observation Setting and Period

During the spring of each study year, each child was observed four times during free play periods in the child care center. Each observation was collected on separate days over a 4-week period. Children were observed in random order. Observations began when a child began to interact with a peer and continued for 5 min whether or not the child continued to interact with peers. Interaction was defined as social behaviors directed to or from the target child and a peer partner or involvement in a mutual game. Social behaviors included smiles, offers, receives, aggression, and talking. A game was defined as mutual involvement in an activity with at least one turn taking interactional structure. The 5-min procedure was adopted to meet two concerns. It was important to sample every child's manner of interaction with peers. Thus observations began only when the child was interacting with a peer. But it was equally important not to overestimate a less sociable child's frequency of peer interaction. Therefore, observations continued for the full 5 min whether or not the child continued to interact with a peer.

Observed Behavior

The observed behaviors selected for study were drawn from four categories: entry, play, affect, and behaviorally identified friends.

Entry.—Every attempt to initiate play with another child was considered an entry behavior. Entry behaviors included verbal utterances, smiles with mutual eye gaze, and object offers. Entry was also coded if parallel activity evolved into a mutual game.

In year 1, *cooperative* entry was coded as the proportion of entries during which the target child smiled, received the object, verbally accepted the invitation to play, or began to play with the initiating child or in which a parallel activity evolved into a mutual game. *Resists* entry in year 1 was coded as the proportion of entries in which the target child ignored the entry behavior, pushed away the offered object, or reacted with physical aggression.

In years 2 and 3 of the study, *easy* entry was coded as the proportion of entries in which either (1) the target child attempted an entry and the partner responded by smiling, accepting the toy, or verbally accepting the invitation to play, (2) parallel activity evolved into a mutual game, or (3) the partner attempted an entry, and the target child smiled and responded by receiving the object, verbally accepted the invitation to play, or began to play with the initiating child (Cronbach Alpha = .98). *Rebuffed* entry was the proportion of entries in which the target child attempted an entry and the partner either ignored the attempt, turned away, verbally rejected the entry, or reacted with physical aggression (Cronbach Alpha = .98).

Play.—Play was coded using the Peer Play Scale (Howes, 1980). *Social play* was the proportion of the observation period during which the child engaged in simple social play (turn-taking play), complementary and reciprocal action, or complementary and reciprocal play (Cronbach Alpha = .96). *Complementary and reciprocal play* was the proportion of play with peers that was rated as complementary and reciprocal on the Peer Play Scale. *Social pretend play* was the proportion of the time that the child engaged in fantasy social play. Fantasy play was defined as any nonliteral activity with or without a partner. *Cooperative social pretend play*, coded only in study years 2 and 3, was the proportion of social pretend play rated as cooperative. Cooperative social pretend play included the use of complementary pretend roles such as bus driver and passenger or mother and baby.

Affect.—Affect was coded in year 1 as the proportion of time that the child engaged in social play with a peer and smiled or laughed. Affect in years 2 and 3 was defined as the proportion of positive affect expressed while engaged in social play with a peer (Cronbach Alpha = .87). Anger and distress also were coded during peer interaction.

Behaviorally identified friends.—In year 1, behaviorally identified friends were identified by the observers on the basis of proximity and shared positive affect. In study years 2 and 3, friends were identified from the code sheets. Behaviorally identified friends maintained proximity and engaged in shared positive affect. Maintained proximity was defined as being within 3 feet of each other during at least 30% of the combined observations of the two children. Shared positive affect was defined as both children expressing positive affect while engaged in social play.

Observation Procedures

Because the first year of data collection was viewed as a time to develop measures that would capture peer interaction over a wide age span, narrative recordings of social behaviors and partner identifications, rather than preselected codes, were used. Interobserver reliability on the narratives was assessed both prior to and during the data collection periods. To establish reliability, each observer recorded the same 10 5-min observations, and the narratives were then independently coded by me and a graduate student assistant for entry, play, and affect. Data collection began when observers attained agreement levels of .85 or higher on the entire narrative. To minimize interobserver drift, interobserver reliability was reestablished at 2-week intervals. In total, 25% of the observations were double coded for the purpose of estimating interobserver reliability. Indices of intercoder reliability were computed using Kappa coefficients (Hollenbeck, 1978) to control for chance agreement. All indices of intercoder reliability were above .89 (range .89–.99).

During the second and third years of the study, observers recorded the presence or absence of 43 preselected behaviors and the identity of the peer partner every 30 sec. The 30-sec time intervals were coded continuously.

Interobserver reliability in the second and third years of the study also was established prior to and during data collection by observers who simultaneously recorded observations. Data collection began when observers reached agreement levels of .80 Kappa coefficients and was reestablished to a .83 Kappa coefficient criterion biweekly. In total, 25% of the observations were double coded for the purpose of estimating interobserver reliability. Interobserver reliabilities on individual variables ranged from .87 to .99 (median = .93).

Classification of Children on the Basis of Social Participation

To supplement the continuous variables provided by measures of observed behaviors, children were classified according to their social participation with peers. The classification system was based on one devised by Rubin (1982) to assess social withdrawal, though the system used here is less stringent than Rubin's because of differences in coding procedures. In the current study, observations of a child did not begin until the child was at least the recipient of peer behavior. Therefore, no child was observed totally isolated from peer contact. In Rubin's work (Rubin, 1982), the coding scheme permitted observing a child with no contact with peers.

Socially *active* children were defined as those children whose social play scores were one or more standard deviations above the mean for their age group. Socially *withdrawn* children were defined as those whose social play scores were one or more standard deviations below the mean for their age group. The remaining children were classified as *average*. Twenty-three percent of the cross-sectional sample was classified as socially active, 8% as socially withdrawn, and 69% as average.

Rated Behaviors

Two sets of rated measures were selected for study. Sociometric ratings were used only in years 2 and 3 of the study and only with those children who had passed their third birthdays. Teacher ratings were identical in all three years of the study and were used on children of all ages.

Sociometric

In the past decade, social scientists have been increasingly concerned with the implications of poor peer relations for social and psychiatric outcomes in later life (Parker & Asher, 1987). Researchers, using social status systems based on sociometric nominations, have found that rejected sociometric status classifications remain relatively stable during middle childhood (Coie & Dodge, 1983). Rejected and neglected sociometric status classifications also discriminate between children's behavioral and cognitive characteristics (Coie & Kupersmidt, 1983; Dodge, 1983; Putallaz, 1983).

Most widely used social status classification systems are based on sociometric nominations (Coie & Dodge, 1983; Newcomb & Bukowski, 1983; Peery, 1979). Sociometric nominations in preschool age children have been criticized for their relatively low reliability, although they have high concurrent validity (Hymel, 1983). An alternative sociometric assessment specifically designed for preschool children is a picture-rating sociometric (Asher et al., 1979). This procedure has acceptable test-retest reliability in preschool samples (Hymel, 1983).

The disadvantage of the sociometric rating method has been that it has failed to differentiate between neglected and rejected children. Recently, Asher and Dodge (1986) devised a classification system based on ratings as well as on nominations that does make this discrimination. High agreement between the Coie and Dodge (1983) classifications, which are based on nominations, and the Asher and Dodge classification system, which is based on ratings, was reported for third- to sixth-grade children. In the current study, I classified children on the basis of sociometric ratings using a modification of the Asher and Dodge (1986) classification system.

Each child 3 years and over completed nomination and rating sociometric measures. Children were asked to identify by name pictures of all children in their class before beginning the sociometric interview. Almost all the children in all classes (median 98%, range 97%–100%) were able to complete this task. The longer hours of contact with peers experienced by the children in the current sample may account for the discrepancy between this result and an earlier report of preschool children's difficulty naming their classmates (Greenwood et al., 1979). The few children who could not identify their classmates were given practice in doing so prior to the sociometric interview.

Nominations.—Nominations were obtained by presenting children with an array of pictures of their classmates and asking them to hand the examiner the pictures of their three best friends and then the pictures of three children who were not their friends.

Ratings.—A modification of the Asher et al. (1979) sociometric measure was used to obtain ratings of sociometric status. The children were given the pictures of their classmates, one by one, and asked to place them in a big, medium, or little bowl according to how much they wanted that person as a friend. Children placed in the big bowl were given a score of 3 and those in the small bowl a score of 1. The test-retest reliabilities of the sociometric procedures will be discussed in a subsequent section of this chapter. The sociometric *rating* score was the average sociometric rating received by each child.

Social status classification.—Children 3 years and older were classified into one of five status groups using a modification of the procedure developed by Asher and Dodge (1986). Classifications were formed as follows. A lowest possible rating (LPR) score was computed as the frequency of 1 ratings (lowest possible rating) received from all peers. The LPR was then standardized across children in a peer group. Up to this point, the procedure in the current study is identical to that used by Asher and Dodge (1986). In the current study, but not in the Asher and Dodge (1986) study, a highest possible rating (HPR) score was computed as the frequency of 3 ratings (highest possible rating) received from all peers. The HPR was also standardized across children in a peer group. The standard scores for the HPR and the LPR were used to generate social preference (Z[HPR] − Z[LPR]) and social impact (Z[HPR] + Z[LPR]) scores. *Popular* children were defined as the group of children who received a social preference score greater than 1.0, an HPR standardized score greater than 0, and an LPR standardized score less than 0. *Rejected* children were defined as the group of children who received a social preference score less than − 1.0, an LPR standardized score greater than 0, and an HPR standardized score less than 0. *Neglected* children were defined as the group of children who received a social impact score less than − 1.0 and LPR and HPR standardized scores less than 0. *Controversial* children were defined as the group of children who received a social impact score greater than 1.0 and HPR and LPR standardized scores each greater than 0. The remaining children were defined as *average.*

According to the rating classification system, 17% of the cross-sectional sample were classified as popular, 13% as rejected, 17% as neglected, and 7% as controversial. Social status classifications were independent of the child's sex and age.

Mutual friendships.—Children 3 years and older were classified into one of three groups based on number of mutual friends. The *no friends* group was defined as children who had no nominated reciprocal friendships, the *one friend* group was defined as children who had only one reciprocal nominated friend, and the *many friends* group was defined as children who had at least two reciprocal nominated friends. Thirty percent of the children had no friends, 42% had one friend, and 28% had many friends.

Teacher ratings

The teacher of each child was asked to complete a Likert-like rating scale for 18 dimensions of that child's functioning with peers. The items on the scale were derived by rewording rating scales designed for use with older children (Baumrind, 1968; Greenwood et al., 1979). Teachers were asked to rate the child relative to children the same age rather than to some ideal standard.

Three composite scores were created to represent social competence with peers. The composite scores were derived by using a principal components analysis to create three empirical clusters of the original 18 items. Cronbach Alpha scores were computed to assess the internal consistency of the cluster.

Three measures emerged from this procedure. *Difficult* was the sum of the following items: is upset easily if a peer interferes with her activities; bosses and dominates other children; hits, pushes, or in other ways hurts other children; reacts with anger if another child takes something that is hers; and is unable to share or take turns (Cronbach Alpha = .93). *Hesitant* was the sum of the following items: withdraws from peer activity; watches rather than participates; and is characteristically shy with peers (Cronbach Alpha = .96). *Sociable* was the sum of the following items: is liked by peers; is the initiator of activities with peers; and shows concern if another child is distressed (Cronbach Alpha = .91). Teachers also nominated three best friends for each child.

Friendship Identification

Each of the 4,154 possible dyads in the study was classified as a nonfriend dyad, a unilateral friend dyad, or a reciprocal friend dyad. Each possible dyad was classified three times on the basis of (1) teacher ratings, (2) sociometric nominations (only children 3 years and older), and (3) behaviorally identified friends. Unilateral friends were defined as dyads in which only one child was nominated. Reciprocal friend dyads were defined as a mutual choice. Using sociometric nominations, 72% of dyads were identified as nonfriends, 20% as unilateral friends, and 8% as reciprocal friends. Approximately the same percent of dyads in each category were identified by the teacher and behavior ratings.[1]

[1] Tables are available from the author on request.

TABLE 4

STABILITY OF OBSERVED BEHAVIORS

Observed Behavior	Median Split-Half Pearson Product-Moment Correlation
Entry:	
Cooperative	.93
Resists	.81
Play:	
Social play	.93
Complementary and reciprocal play	.91
Social pretend	.82
Affect: Positive	.92

	OBSERVATION	
	1	2
Entry:		
Easy	.79	.82
Rebuff	.85	.83
Play:		
Social	.85	.87
Complementary and reciprocal	.93	.86
Social pretend	.79	.83
Cooperative social pretend	.77	.86
Affect	.64	.73
Behavior friends	.70	.78

STABILITY OF OBSERVED BEHAVIORS AND SOCIOMETRIC MEASURES

The stability of the observed measures (entry, play, affect, and behaviorally identified friends) was estimated by computing split-half reliability estimates on the 20 min of observation per child. The split-half reliability figures for years 1, 2, and 3 of the study are presented in Table 4. Observed behaviors were moderately to highly stable. Measures of social skill (i.e., entry behaviors, complementary and reciprocal peer play, and cooperative social pretend play) were more stable than measures of affect.

The reliability of the sociometric measures was assessed by test-retest reliability for 25% of the children of each age sampled (year 2, $N = 82$; year 3, $N = 48$). Reliability estimates are presented in Table 5. Test-retest stability ranged between .54 and .77 for nominations and between .76 and .84 for ratings. Test-retest reliability for rating measures was higher than for nomination measures, and reliability increased with age between 3 and 6 years. The reliability of sociometric nominations for preschool children obtained in the current study was higher than that usually reported (Hymel, 1983).

TABLE 5

TEST-RETEST RELIABILITY OF SOCIOMETRIC MEASURES

| | AGE IN YEARS | | | |
MEASURE	3	4	5	6
Positive nominations[a]	.54	.69	.75	.77
Negative nominations[a]	.57	.64	.73	.76
Rating[b]	.76	.78	.81	.84

[a] Median Kappa coefficients of agreement for individual selections.
[b] Pearson product-moment correlations between scores time 1 and time 2.

AGREEMENT BETWEEN FRIENDSHIP IDENTIFICATION METHODS

Agreement between teacher, sociometric, and behavioral methods of identification of friendship dyads was examined by computing chi squares between methods. Teacher and sociometric nominations were in agreement for 78% of the dyads, $\chi^2(4) = 346.84, p < .001$. Eighty-seven percent of the disagreements were between reciprocal and unilateral friendships. There was more agreement between teacher and sociometric nominations in the 3-year-old group than in the 4–6-year-old group, $\chi^2(1) = 7.35, p < .01$.

Behaviorally identified friends and sociometric nominations were in agreement for 72% of dyads, $\chi^2(2) = 98.29, p < .001$. Eighty-nine percent of the disagreements occurred because a behaviorally identified friend received a unilateral sociometric nomination. There was more agreement between behaviorally identified friends and sociometric nominations for the 3-year-olds than for the 4–6-year-olds, $\chi^2(1) = 6.39, p < .01$.

Behaviorally identified friends and teacher nominations were in agreement for 85% of the dyads, $\chi^2(2) = 129.27, p < .001$. Ninety percent of the disagreements consisted of a behaviorally identified friend receiving a unilateral teacher nomination. There was more agreement between behaviorally identified friends and teacher nominations for 1- and 2-year-olds than for children 3 years old and older, $\chi^2(1) = 5.73, p < .05$.

SUMMARY AND DISCUSSION

The major question of this chapter concerns the reliability of the measures used to assess social competence with peers. Not surprisingly, the observed social behaviors were more reliable than the sociometric ratings. Children in the current study engaged in relatively stable social behaviors. Easy entry into play groups, complementary and reciprocal peer play, cooperative social pretend play, and behavioral friends ranged in stability from .70 to .91 across observational sessions.

Children were less able to make reliable sociometric nominations. The test-retest reliability of sociometric nominations was not sufficiently high to justify forming social status classifications. However, the children could reliably make sociometric ratings. The test-retest reliability of the sociometric ratings was acceptable and was used to form both a rating score and a social status classification for each child.

The test-retest reliability of both the sociometric nominations and the sociometric ratings was higher than previously reported for nursery school children (Hymel, 1983) and comparable to that reported in a recently published study of child care children (Poteat, Ironsmith, & Bullock, 1986). Differences between the social experiences of children in these two settings may account for the relative stability of child care children's sociometric nominations. The child care children spend the majority of their waking hours in the company of a relatively small number of peers. Many of the children had been with the same peer group since infancy. Few children failed to identify all the pictures of classmates. Observers reported that the children reacted as if the task were silly—how could the grown-up not know all the children. In contrast, children in traditional nursery school settings spend a few hours per day several days a week with their peer group. Peers are a less important part of their lives, and thus their sociometric nominations may be less reliable.

Child care attendance appears to stimulate social cognitive development, possibly because the children encounter more variations in social experiences in child care than they do in traditional families (Clarke-Stewart, 1983). The general acceleration of social cognitive abilities may be reflected in increased stability of sociometric nominations.

Teacher nomination, behavioral identification, and sociometric nomination methods of identifying friendship tended to agree. Teachers' friendship nominations were less consistent with behavioral friendship identifications in the older groups than they were in the younger groups. Infants and toddlers have been reported to have a limited number of maintained friendships, while preschoolers have a wider range of less stable friendships (Howes, 1983). Therefore, friendships in the infant/toddler period may be more salient to the teachers than friendships in the preschool period. Agreement between behavioral and sociometric identification of friendships also decreased with age. Studies of the social cognition of friendship (e.g., Furman & Bierman, 1983) suggest that, with age, children differentiate playmates from intimate associates. Therefore, younger children may have been more likely than older children to nominate their frequent playmates as sociometric friends. Likewise, the greater communicative ability of the older children may have permitted them to play in a friendly manner with children who were not their friends.

In summary, the selected behavioral measures of social competence with peers—entry into play groups, play, and affect—were stable over the 4-week observation period. Sociometric ratings were reasonably stable over a 2-week period. Teachers, peers, and observers agreed when identifying mutual friends.

III. DEVELOPMENTAL SEQUENCES

Chapter III examines developmental sequences in social competence with peers. Complementary and reciprocal play with peers was expected to represent social competence in the early toddler period. Cooperative social pretend play was expected to represent social competence in the late toddler period (see Table 1). Complementary and reciprocal play was expected to emerge before cooperative social pretend play.

The proportions of both types of play were compared across the age groups included in the sample to test these hypotheses. It was hypothesized that there would be higher proportions of complementary and reciprocal peer play in the preschool (ages 4–6) than in the toddler period (ages 1–3) and that the proportion of complementary and reciprocal peer play would increase between the early toddler (age 1) and the late toddler periods (ages 2 and 3). Complementary and reciprocal play was not expected to increase in proportion during the late toddler or preschool periods.

It was further hypothesized that cooperative social pretend play would increase in proportion between the late toddler (ages 2 and 3) and the preschool (ages 4–6) periods but not during the preschool period.

Sex differences in observed and rated behaviors also are explored in this chapter. Data from the cross-sectional sample were used in these analyses.

COMPLEMENTARY AND RECIPROCAL PEER PLAY

Cross-sectional Analysis

Analysis of variance was used to compare the proportion of both complementary and reciprocal peer play and cooperative social pretend play by age, sex, and their interaction using the cross-sectional sample. Dunn's procedure (Kirk, 1982, pp. 106–109, 128–129) was used as a post hoc technique to exert control over the conceptual error rate. Fifteen contrasts were

TABLE 6

COMPARISON OF PROPORTIONS OF PLAY WITH PEERS
IN THE CROSS-SECTIONAL SAMPLE

| | DEVELOPMENTAL PERIOD | | | | | | |
| | Early Toddler[a] | | Late Toddler[b] | | Preschool[c] | | |
PLAY	M	SD	M	SD	M	SD	F
Complementary and reciprocal ..	.04	.07	.18	.13	.35	.24	24.42***
Cooperative	.09	.23	.21	.17	.41	.34	10.81***

[a] 13–24 months.
[b] 2–3 years.
[c] 4–6 years.
*** $p < .001$.

made. In this and all other portions of the results sections, only significant comparisons are reported.

The proportions of complementary and reciprocal peer play in the early and late toddler and preschool periods of development in the cross-sectional sample are presented in Table 6. As predicted, the proportion of complementary and reciprocal peer play was higher in the late toddler period than in the early toddler period, $tD(320) = 2.97, p < .05$, and higher in the preschool period than in the toddler periods, $tD(320) = 3.06, p < .05$.

Longitudinal Analysis

Changes in the proportion of complementary and reciprocal peer play over time in the combined longitudinal samples are presented in Table 7. The significance of these changes was tested by dependent t tests. Complementary and reciprocal peer play increased between the early and late toddler periods but not within the late toddler or preschool periods.

COOPERATIVE SOCIAL PRETEND PLAY

Cross-sectional Analysis

The proportion of cooperative social pretend play in the early and late toddler and preschool periods of development in the cross-sectional sample is also presented in Table 6. As predicted, the proportion of cooperative social pretend play increased from the late toddler to the preschool periods, $tD(320) = 3.02, p < .05$.

TABLE 7

COMPARISON OF FREQUENCIES OF PLAY WITH PEERS IN THE COMBINED
LONGITUDINAL SAMPLE

| | TIME | | | | |
| | 1 | | 2 | | |
AGE	M	SD	M	SD	t
Complementary and reciprocal:					
Early toddler (1 year)	.03	.01	.19	.12	3.63**
Late toddler (2–3 years)	.21	.16	.29	.25	1.51
Preschool (4–6 years)	.31	.27	.36	.31	.87
Cooperative social pretend:					
Early toddler (1 year)	.10	.03	.19	.11	1.39
Late toddler (2–3 years)	.13	.08	.40	.21	2.15**
Preschool (4–6 years)	.46	.12	.55	.32	.51

** $p < .01$.

Longitudinal Analysis

Changes, again assessed by dependent t tests, in the proportion of cooperative social pretend play over time in the combined longitudinal samples are also presented in Table 7. Cooperative social pretend play increased between the late toddler period and the preschool period but not during the preschool period.

SEX DIFFERENCES IN MEASURES OF SOCIAL COMPETENCY WITH PEERS

Sex differences and the interaction of sex and age were examined by analyses of variance using Dunn's procedure for 15 contrasts. Teacher ratings of difficulty with peers were higher for boys than for girls, $tD(329) = 3.16$, $p < .05$. Ratings of sociability were higher for girls than for boys, $tD(329) = 3.24$, $p < .05$.

SUMMARY AND DISCUSSION

The analyses reported in this chapter support the hypothesized sequence of qualitative changes in social competence with peers. In both the cross-sectional and the longitudinal samples, complementary and reciprocal play emerged in the early toddler period and increased with age. Cooperative social pretend play in both samples emerged in the late toddler period and increased with age. Both complementary and reciprocal social play and cooperative social pretend play tended to level off in the preschool period.

These findings are consistent with previous studies that have reported increases in elaborated exchanges and sustained play with peers from the toddler to the preschool periods (Holmberg, 1980; Jacobson & Wille, 1986). Cooperative social pretend play is less complex than the social pretend play of preschoolers investigated by Connolly and Doyle (1984) and Garvey (1977). If I had used a more complex measure of social pretend play, I would have expected further developmental changes in social pretend play during the preschool period.

Future research is necessary to test alternative representations of competence proposed in the current research. These behavioral constructs are measures of positive or successful social interaction. I have assumed that all children will engage in these behaviors, given reasonably favorable circumstances. Alternative clusters of behavior might be constructed to predict maladaptive behavior with peers. For example, measures could be constructed to capture early social withdrawal from peers or early aversive behavior with peers. Subsequent research could test these alternative behavior clusters against those proposed in the current study.

In summary, the findings suggest there are qualitative developmental changes in social competence with peers across the early toddler to preschool periods of development. As predicted, these changes are represented in complementary and reciprocal peer play and cooperative social pretend play.

IV. INDIVIDUAL DIFFERENCES WITHIN PERIODS

In Chapter IV, I test the assumption that the behavioral construct selected to represent social competence within a developmental period corresponds to individual differences in alternative measures of social competence. Specifically, I hypothesize that the relative proportion of social play that is complementary and reciprocal defines individual differences during the early toddler period. Similarly, I hypothesize that the relative proportion of social pretend play that is cooperative defines individual differences during the late toddler period and that sociometric ratings define individual differences during the preschool period.

I tested these assumptions by examining associations among the behavioral constructs, children's entry behaviors, and teacher ratings. Teacher ratings of sociability and easy entries were expected to be related to the proportion of complementary and reciprocal social play, to the proportion of cooperative social pretend play, and to sociometric ratings.

INTERCORRELATIONS BETWEEN MEASURES

One strength of this study was that multiple methods were used to assess children's social competence with peers. Using the cross-sectional sample, relations between measures were computed using Pearson product-moment correlations. Interrelations between observed behaviors, between teacher ratings and observed behavior, between sociometric ratings and observed behavior, and, finally, between sociometric and teacher ratings are discussed.

Observed Behavior

Observed behaviors indicative of social competence with peers (easy and cooperative entry, complementary peer play, and social pretend play) within each age group were moderately correlated with each other.[2]

[2] Tables are available from the author on request.

Teacher Ratings and Observed Behavior

Relations between observed behaviors and teacher ratings are presented in Table 8. Teacher ratings of sociability with peers correlated moderately to highly with observed play behaviors. These correlations decreased in strength with the children's age. Teacher ratings of difficulty with peers correlated moderately with observed difficult entry in the younger age groups but not in the 4–6-year-olds. Teacher ratings of hesitant behavior with peers correlated moderately with play behaviors for only the youngest age groups.

Sociometric Ratings and Observed Behavior

Relations between observed behavior and the standardized sociometric rating are presented in Table 9. Ratings in both age groups correlated moderately with measures of easy entry and of play.

Sociometric and Teacher Ratings

Positive sociometric ratings correlated moderately and positively with teacher ratings of sociability in both 3-year-olds, $r(54) = .37$, $p < .01$, and 4–6-year-olds, $r(194) = .24$, $p > .01$, and negatively with difficulty with peers in both 3-year-olds, $r(54) = -.22$, $p < .01$, and 4–6-year-olds, $r(194) = -.25$, $p < .01$. Positive sociometric ratings correlated negatively with teacher ratings of hesitancy with peers in 3-year-olds, $r(56) = -.29$, $p < .05$, but not in 4–6-year-olds, $r(196) = .08$.

RELATIONS BETWEEN CLASSIFICATION SYSTEMS

Relations between social status, mutual friend, and social participation classification systems also were examined. As discussed in Chapter I, the constructs that underlie these classification systems—popularity, friendship, and social participation—are conceptually independent. Therefore, I expected low to moderate associations between classification systems.

SOCIAL STATUS AND SOCIAL PARTICIPATION CLASSIFICATIONS

Relations between social status based on rated behavior and social participation based on observed behaviors were also assessed.[3] Chi-square anal-

---

[3] Tables are available from the author on request.

TABLE 8

Relations between Observed Behaviors and Teacher Ratings

	Teacher Ratings		
Observed Behavior	Difficult	Hesitant	Sociable
Longitudinal sample 1:[a]			
Entry:			
Cooperative	−.09	−.02	.79**
Resists	.22	.13	−.16
Play:			
Social	.05	−.52**	.76**
Complementary	−.16	−.14	.78**
Social pretend	−.22	−.31*	.53**
Affect	−.22	−.05	.18
Cross-sectional sample:			
Early toddler:[b]			
Entry:			
Easy	−.28*	−.18	.16
Rebuff	.24*	−.34**	−.08
Play:			
Social	−.32**	−.29**	.35**
Complementary	−.21**	−.31**	.67**
Social pretend	−.19	−.28**	.61**
Cooperative	−.11	−.21*	.12
Affect	−.17	−.18	.26*
2- and 3-year-olds:[c]			
Entry:			
Easy	.01	−.13	.24*
Rebuff	.31**	−.07	.02
Play:			
Social	−.07	−.13	.24*
Complementary	−.29*	−.13	.07
Social pretend	−.30**	−.12	.09
Cooperative	−.26*	−.13	.30**
Affect	−.19*	.04	.24*
4–6-year-olds:[d]			
Entry:			
Easy	.03	−.12	.01
Rebuff	−.04	−.01	−.07
Play:			
Social	−.16*	−.07	.07
Complementary	−.05	−.20*	.18*
Social pretend	−.04	−.22*	.29**
Cooperative	−.19*	.19*	.38**
Affect	−.11	−.09	.25**

[a] 16–33 months, $N = 43$.
[b] 13–24 months, $N = 34$.
[c] $N = 99$.
[d] $N = 196$.
* $p < .05$.
** $p < .01$.

TABLE 9

RELATIONS BETWEEN OBSERVED BEHAVIORS
AND SOCIOMETRIC RATINGS

Observed Behavior	Sociometric Rating
3-year-olds:[a]	
Entry:	
Easy	.34**
Rebuff	−.26*
Play:	
Social	.39**
Complementary	.49**
Social pretend	.51**
Cooperative	.52**
Affect	.13
4–6-year-olds:[b]	
Entry:	
Easy	.66**
Rebuff	−.19*
Play:	
Social	.24**
Complementary	.48**
Social pretend	.41**
Cooperative	.44**
Affect	.18*

[a] $N = 56$. [b] $N = 196$. * $p \leq .05$. ** $p \leq .01$.

yses, $\chi^2(8) = 4.14$, N.S., indicated that the social status and social participation classification systems were independent.

Mutual Friend, Social Status, and Social Participation Classifications

Relations between social status and mutual friend classification systems are presented in Table 10. Chi-square analysis, $\chi^2(8) = 24.49$, $p < .01$, indicated that the mutual friend and the social status classification systems were associated. Despite the association between systems, some children of every social status classification, including neglected and rejected, had mutual friends.

Relations between social participation and the mutual friend classification systems are also presented in Table 10. Chi-square analysis indicated that the two systems were independent, $\chi^2(4) = .44$, N.S.

SUMMARY AND DISCUSSION

I hypothesized that complementary and reciprocal social play represented social competence with peers in the early toddler period (see Table 1

TABLE 10

RELATIONS BETWEEN MUTUAL FRIEND, SOCIAL STATUS, AND SOCIAL
PARTICIPATION CLASSIFICATIONS[a]

| | MUTUAL FRIEND | | |
CLASSIFICATION	None	One	Many
Social status:			
Popular	0	16	44
Rejected	52	7	7
Neglected	20	23	0
Controversial	5	18	4
Average	23	48	41
Social participation:			
Active	7	34	34
Average	36	51	56
Withdrawn	57	15	10

[a] Numbers in table represent percent of mutual friend classification; chi-square analyses were conducted on actual frequencies.

and Chap. I). The analyses reported in the current chapter support this hypothesis. Complementary and reciprocal social play was positively associated with cooperative entry, easy entry, and teacher ratings of sociability in the early toddler period.

Similarly, I hypothesized that cooperative social pretend play represented social competence with peers in the late toddler period (see Table 1 and Chap. I). Again, the analyses reported in the current chapter support this hypothesis. Cooperative social pretend play associated positively with easy entry and teacher ratings of sociability in the late toddler period.

Finally, I hypothesized that sociometric ratings were related to individual differences in social competence with peers in the preschool period. The analyses reported in the current chapter also support this hypothesis. Sociometric ratings associated positively with teacher ratings of sociability and negatively with teacher ratings of difficulty with peers. However, teacher ratings of hesitancy with peers associated only negatively with sociometric ratings in the younger group of preschoolers. This last finding is inconsistent with reports by Rubin (1982, 1985; Rubin & Clark, 1983) that withdrawal from peers becomes increasingly salient with age. Specifically, Rubin and Clark (1983) report strong associations between preschool sociometric ratings and teacher ratings of anxiety and fearfulness. This discrepancy may arise from the teacher rating scale used in the current study. My scale did not include global anxiety and fearfulness. The discrepancy may also be due to differences between teacher ratings of hesitancy with peers and observations of solitude or nonsocial play as definitions of social withdrawal.

I attempted to make the items applicable to children across the wide age span of the study. Therefore, the ratings may be less able to capture the more sophisticated nuances of behavior in the oldest age group. Furthermore, unlike the current study, Rubin and Clark's (1983) teacher ratings of anxiety and fearfulness were not specific to peer relationships. Generalized fear and anxiety may be more strongly associated with negative sociometric ratings than with specific hesitancy with peers. This may be because a child is more likely to receive low ratings for being disliked by peers than for being socially withdrawn from peers.

More generally, the current study replicated a series of experimental and observational studies in which associations between sociometric ratings and observed social skills in peer interaction were found (Coie & Kupersmidt, 1983; Dodge, 1983; Hartup, 1983; Rubin & Daniels-Beirness, 1983). Sociometric ratings positively associated with easy entry, social play, complementary and reciprocal play, social pretend play, and cooperative social pretend play. The current study extends previous research by identifying measures of social competence (complementary and reciprocal social play and cooperative social pretend play) in toddler age children. These indicators of social competence could be useful in designing assessment and intervention programs for young children.

As predicted, children's classifications on the basis of popularity (sociometric ratings) were independent of their classifications on the basis of social participation. This finding is consistent with previous research on socially withdrawn children and supports the premise that children classified as rejected, neglected, or socially withdrawn exhibit different patterns of behavior (Rubin, 1982, 1985; Rubin, Hymel, LeMare, & Rowden, in press).

Furthermore, in the current study, children's classifications on the basis of popularity (sociometric ratings) were moderately independent of their classifications on the basis of reciprocated friendship (mutual friends). No child classified as popular was without mutual friends. Children classified as rejected were most likely to have no mutual friends, although a few of these children had mutual friends. These findings support the assumption discussed in Chapter I that friendship and social skills, at least as assessed by sociometric ratings, are related yet independent aspects of social competence with peers.

There were strong associations between individual differences in behavioral constructs predicted to represent social competence in young children (complementary and reciprocal play, cooperative social pretend play, and sociometric rating) and more established indicators of individual differences in social competence with peers (ease of entry into peer groups and teacher ratings). These findings support the assumption that individual differences in the identified behavioral constructs of each period do represent individual differences in social competence with peers.

The major question in Chapter V concerns the stability of social competence with peers across developmental periods. Individual differences in social competence during one period were expected to be associated with individual differences in subsequent periods. Specifically, the proportion of complementary and reciprocal peer play observed during the early toddler period (13–24 months) was expected to predict the proportion of cooperative social pretend play in the late toddler period (2- and 3-year-olds). The proportion of cooperative social pretend play in the late toddler period was expected to predict sociometric and teacher ratings in preschool.

I also explored the stability of individual behaviors, teacher ratings, and social classifications over 2- and 3-year time periods (longitudinal samples 2 and 3, respectively). Individual differences in particular behaviors that represent social competence within a period were not expected to be stable across periods. That is, children high in complementary and reciprocal peer play in one period were not expected necessarily to be high in that form of play in a subsequent period. These behaviors represent accomplishments of a particular developmental period rather than an orientation toward peers.

I expected individual differences in other observed behaviors, particularly social play and affect, to remain relatively stable over a 2- or 3-year period. These behaviors represent an orientation toward peers rather than competence. I expected children's social status and social participation classifications to be relatively unstable during the preschool years. This hypothesis was based on previous findings (Hymel, 1983; Rubin, 1982, 1985).

PREDICTION OF PRESCHOOL SOCIAL COMPETENCE WITH PEERS

Constructs representing social competence in one period were predicted from measures of competence collected in a previous period in order to test the hypothesis of stability of social competence across developmental periods. Predictive relations were tested in two ways. First, partial correlations removing chronological age were computed between behavior in time 1 and the construct hypothesized to represent competence in time 2. Chronological age was removed from the relation because each age group of children contained at least a 12-month age span. Next, two-step multiple regression equations were computed using the construct representing competence in time 2 as the dependent variable and chronological age and behaviors in time 1 as the predictor variables. In each regression procedure, chronological age was entered into the equation first; then the time 1 behaviors were entered in stepwise fashion.

Prediction of Cooperative Social Pretend Play

The predictability of individual differences in observed behaviors during the early toddler period (13–24 months) for cooperative social pretend play in the late toddler period (2- and 3-year-olds) was examined to test the hypothesis that social competence with peers is stable between the early and the late toddler periods. Partial correlations, computed separately for longitudinal samples 1 and 2, are presented in Table 11. As predicted, in both samples, the proportion of complementary and reciprocal peer play in the

TABLE 11

RELATIONS BETWEEN COOPERATIVE SOCIAL PRETEND PLAY IN THE LATE TODDLER PERIOD AND EARLIER OBSERVED BEHAVIOR IN THE LONGITUDINAL SAMPLES[a]

Observed Behavior, Early Toddler Period[b]	Cooperative Social Pretend Play, Late Toddler Period[c]
Longitudinal sample 1:	
Entry:	
Cooperative	.05
Resists	−.03
Play:	
Social	.21
Complementary and reciprocal	.75**
Social pretend	.32*
Affect	.11
Longitudinal sample 2:	
Entry:	
Easy	.14
Rebuff	.19
Play:	
Social	.36**
Complementary and reciprocal	.66**
Social pretend	.39**
Cooperative	.35**
Affect	.17

[a] Partial correlations with age removed.   [b] 13–24 months.   [c] 2- and 3-year-olds.   * $p < .05$.   ** $p < .01$.

early toddler period was highly related to the proportion of cooperative social pretend play in the late toddler period across both samples. The only other association with cooperative social pretend play that appeared in both samples was social pretend play.

In both longitudinal samples, complementary and reciprocal peer play was the only observed behavior to contribute significantly to the variance after chronological age (chronological age plus complementary and reciprocal play: sample 1, $R = .84$, $R^2 = .71$, $F[2,41] = 5.31$, $p < .01$; sample 2, $R = .77$, $R^2 = .59$, $F[2,32] = 5.43$, $p < .01$).

Prediction of Preschool Sociometric Ratings

Observed Behaviors.—Cooperative social pretend play in the late toddler period was hypothesized to predict sociometric rating in preschool. The partial correlations are presented in Table 12. In both samples, cooperative social pretend play in the late toddler period was associated with sociometric ratings in preschool. Relations between observed behavior in the preschool period and sociometric rating 1 year later are also presented in Table 12. As expected, there were no strong relations. The strongest association was with ease of entry into play groups.

In longitudinal sample 1 and in the toddler sample of longitudinal sample 2, cooperative social pretend play was the first and only observed

TABLE 12

RELATIONS BETWEEN SOCIOMETRIC RATING IN PRESCHOOL AND EARLIER OBSERVED BEHAVIOR IN THE LONGITUDINAL SAMPLES[a]

OBSERVED BEHAVIORS, TIME 1	PRESCHOOL SOCIOMETRIC RATING, TIME 2		
	28–45 Months[b]	2- and 3- Year-Olds[c]	4- and 5- Year-Olds[c]
Entry:			
Easy	.17	.02	.23
Rebuff	−.02	−.15	.05
Play:			
Social	.10	.16	.13
Complementary and reciprocal	.33*	.29**	.02
Social pretend	.26	.21*	.01
Cooperative social pretend	.72**	.64**	.01
Affect	.12	.19	.11

[a] Partial correlations with age removed.
[b] Longitudinal sample 1, age time 1.
[c] Longitudinal sample 2, age time 1.
* $p \leq .05$.
** $p \leq .01$.

TABLE 13

Relations between Sociometric Rating and Earlier Teacher Ratings
in the Longitudinal Samples[a]

Teacher Ratings, Time 1	Preschool Sociometric Rating, Time 2			
	16–33 Months[b]	28–45 Months[b]	2- and 3- Year-Olds[c]	4- and 5- Year-Olds[c]
Difficult	−.19	−.18	−.23*	−.20
Hesitant	−.11	−.07	−.05	−.11
Sociable	.70**	.57**	.48**	.40**

[a] Partial correlations with age removed.
[b] Longitudinal sample 1, age time 1.
[c] Longitudinal sample 2, age time 1.
* $p \leq .05$.
** $p \leq .01$.

behavior to contribute significantly to the variance after chronological age (chronological age plus cooperative social pretend play: sample 1, $R = .68$, $R^2 = .46$, $F[2,41] = 5.64$, $p < .01$; sample 2, $R = .62$, $R^2 = .39$, $F[2,97] = 4.12$, $p < .01$). In the preschool sample of longitudinal sample 2, easy entry was the first and only observed behavior to contribute significantly to the variance after chronological age (chronological age plus easy entry: sample 2, $R = .35$, $R^2 = .12$, $F[2,194] = 3.17$, $p < .05$).

Teacher ratings.—Relations between teacher ratings and subsequent sociometric ratings were also examined using partial correlations. These are presented in Table 13. Teacher ratings of sociability with peers in the early toddler period, the late toddler period, and the preschool period were associated with preschool sociometric ratings.

In both samples and in each period tested, teacher ratings of sociability were the first and only predictor to contribute significantly to the variance following chronological age (chronological age plus sociability: sample 1 between times 1 and 3: $R = .61$, $R^2 = .37$, $F[2,41] = 5.28$, $p < .01$; sample 1 between times 2 and 3: $R = .52$, $R^2 = .27$, $F[2,41] = 5.21$, $p < .01$; sample 2, toddler: $R = .47$, $R^2 = .22$, $F[2,69] = 5.03$, $p < .01$; sample 2, preschool: $R = .42$, $R^2 = .18$, $F[2,116] = 4.87$, $p < .01$).

Prediction of Preschool Teacher Ratings from Observed Behavior

Relations between earlier observed behaviors and preschool teacher ratings were examined as an alternative assessment of the hypothesis that early social behaviors predict preschool social competence with peers. Again, partial correlations with age removed and two-step multiple regression equations were used. Partial correlations are presented in Table 14. As

TABLE 14

RELATIONS BETWEEN PRESCHOOL TEACHER RATINGS AND EARLIER OBSERVED BEHAVIOR
IN THE LONGITUDINAL SAMPLES

| | PRESCHOOL TEACHER RATINGS | | |
OBSERVED BEHAVIOR	Difficult	Hesitant	Sociable
Sample 1:			
Early toddler:[a]			
Entry:			
Cooperative	−.31*	−.22	.27
Resist	.04	.54**	.07
Play:			
Social	−.09	−.05	.40**
Complementary and reciprocal	.02	.14	.49**
Social pretend	.10	.06	.21
Affect	−.02	.17	.26
Late toddler:[b]			
Entry:			
Easy	.10	−.22	.16
Rebuff	.21	.17	−.14
Play:			
Social	−.22	−.10	.32*
Complementary and reciprocal	.25	−.34*	.40**
Social pretend	−.20	−.18	.36*
Cooperative	−.52**	−.38*	.54**
Affect	−.02	−.10	.49**
Sample 2:			
Early toddler:[c]			
Entry:			
Easy	−.32**	−.43**	.44**
Rebuff	.51**	.23*	.30**
Play:			
Social	−.28*	−.01	.24*
Complementary and reciprocal	.18	−.44**	.45**
Social pretend	.15	−.42**	.21*
Cooperative	.13	−.23	.31**
Affect	−.15	.03	.25**
Late toddler:[d]			
Entry:			
Easy	−.22*	.04	.39**
Rebuff	.27*	.06	−.08
Play:			
Social	−.04	−.19	.24*
Complementary and reciprocal	−.32**	.12	.26*
Social pretend	.27*	−.08	.20
Cooperative	−.23*	−.20	.49**
Affect	.10	−.34**	.44**
Preschool:[e]			
Entry:			
Easy	−.32**	−.22*	.21*
Rebuff	.27**	.01	−.18
Play:			
Social	−.08	−.08	.10
Complementary and reciprocal	−.11	.14	.03
Social pretend	−.10	−.23*	.24*
Cooperative	−.32**	−.16	.35**
Affect	−.10	−.41**	.63**

[a] $N = 42$.
[b] $N = 41$.
[c] 1 year, $N = 34$.
[d] 2–3 years, $N = 71$.
[e] 4–6 years, $N = 118$.
* $p \le .05$.
** $p \le .01$.

expected, complementary and reciprocal peer play in the early toddler period had the strongest relation with teacher ratings of sociability with peers in the late toddler period and in the preschool period. Also as expected, cooperative social pretend play in the late toddler period had the strongest relation with sociability with peers in the preschool period. Positive affect with peers in the preschool period had the strongest relation with teacher ratings of sociability with peers in the subsequent year.

The positive association between teacher ratings of sociability and rebuffed entry in the early toddler subsample of longitudinal sample 2 was unexpected. One post hoc explanation is that teachers were aware that children who were receiving rebuffs from peers were engaged with peers and so rated them as sociable without discriminating between positive and negative interactions.

Complementary and reciprocal play was the only observed behavior to contribute significantly to the variance following chronological age when predicting teacher ratings in the late toddler period (chronological age plus complementary and reciprocal play: sample 1, $R = .42, R^2 = .18, F[2,41] = 5.26, p < .01$; sample 2, $R = .54, R^2 = .29, F[2,32] = 5.44, p < .01$). Cooperative social pretend play was the only observed behavior to contribute significantly to the variance following chronological age when predicting teacher ratings of sociability between the late toddler and the preschool periods (chronological age plus cooperative social pretend: sample 1, $R = .47, R^2 = .22, F[2,41] = 5.39, p < .01$; sample 2, $R = .43, R^2 = .19, F[2,69] = 5.01, p < .01$). Positive affect was the only observed behavior to contribute significantly to the variance following chronological age when predicting teacher ratings of sociability within the preschool period, $R = .54, R^2 = .29, F(2,116) = 4.86, p < .01$.

Teacher ratings of difficulty in the late toddler period were predicted in sample 1 only by the lack of cooperative responses to entry (chronological age minus cooperative entry: $R = .29, R^2 = .08, F[2,41] = 3.25, p < .05$) and in sample 2 only by rebuff (chronological age plus rebuff: $R = .47, R^2 = .22, F[2,32] = 3.36, p < .05$). Teacher ratings of difficulty in the preschool period were predicted by poor peer play skills in the late toddler period. In sample 1, lack of cooperative social pretend play (chronological age minus cooperative social pretend: $R = .41, R^2 = .17, F[2,41] = 5.24, p < .01$), and, in sample 2, lack of complementary and reciprocal play (chronological age minus complementary and reciprocal play: $R = .29, R^2 = .08, F[2,69] = 3.34, p < .05$) were the first and only predictors to follow chronological age in predicting difficulty ratings. Within the preschool sample, lack of easy entry was the first and only predictor to follow chronological age in predicting difficulty ratings (chronological age minus easy entry: $R = .29, R^2 = .08, F[2,116] = 3.09, p < .05$).

Teacher ratings of hesitancy with peers in the late toddler period were predicted from early toddler behaviors only by resistance in sample 1 (chronological age plus resist: $R = .46, R^2 = .21, F[2,41] = 5.22, p < .01$) and by lack of complementary and reciprocal play in sample 2 (chronological age minus complementary and reciprocal play: $R = .31, R^2 = .10, F[2,32] = 3.39, p < .05$). Teacher ratings of hesitancy with peers in the preschool period were predicted by lack of cooperative social pretend play in sample 1 (chronological age minus cooperative social pretend: late toddler to preschool, $R = .36, R^2 = .13, F[2,41] = 3.27, p < .05$) and by low positive affect in sample 2 (chronological age minus affect: late toddler to preschool, $R = .29, R^2 = .08, F[2,69] = 3.21, p < .05$; preschool to preschool, $R = .34, R^2 = .12, F[2,116] = 3.09, p < .05$).

STABILITY OF INDIVIDUAL BEHAVIORS AND RATINGS

Observed Behaviors

Changes and stability in observed behaviors over time were examined by partial correlations removing chronological age and are presented in Table 15. The relations were computed separately for children in the early (1-year-olds) and late (2- and 3-year-olds) toddler periods and in the preschool period (4- and 5-year-olds).

Individual differences in observed behaviors were moderately stable over a 1-year and a 2-year period. As predicted, individual differences in behaviors representing an orientation toward peers (social play and affect) were generally more stable than behaviors representing competence (complementary and reciprocal peer play and cooperative social pretend play). However, even the most stable of observed behaviors had a reliability estimate of only .62.

Teacher Ratings

The stability of teacher ratings of children's social competence with peers, as computed by partial correlations removing the effect of age, is presented in Table 16. The relations were computed separately for children in the early and late toddler periods and in the preschool period. Relations were moderately stable and tended to increase in stability as the children reached the preschool period.

Sociometric Ratings

Sociometric rating as computed by partial correlations over a 1-year period was modestly stable in both samples: sample 1, $r(35) = .40, p < .01$; sample 2, $r(153) = .38, p < .01$.

Classifications

Social status.—Social status classification remained moderately stable over a year, $\chi^2(16) = 31.57$, $p < .01$.[4] Sixty percent of popular, 60% of rejected, 33% of neglected, 80% of controversial, and 65% of average children had stable classifications. Neglected children were more likely than the other children to change their classification, $\chi^2(4) = 13.72$, $p < .05$.

Social participation.—Social participation classifications were unstable over a year period, $\chi^2(4) = 4.39$, N.S.[5] Thirty-eight percent of socially active, 41% of average, and 74% of socially withdrawn children changed their classifications. Socially active children and average children were more likely than socially withdrawn children to maintain their social participation classifications, $\chi^2(2) = 6.14$, $p < .05$.

Mutual friend.—Mutual friend classifications were also not stable between years 2 and 3 of the study, $\chi^2(4) = 1.11$, N.S.[6] Seventy-four percent of children with no friends, 60% with one friend, and 47% with many friends changed their classification. Children with many friends were most likely to maintain stable mutual friend classifications, $\chi^2(2) = 7.02$, $p < .05$.

SUMMARY AND DISCUSSION

Individual differences in clusters of behaviors that represent social competence within a period were expected to predict individual differences in the clusters of behaviors that represent social competence within a subsequent period. The analyses presented in this chapter support this hypothesis. Complementary and reciprocal social play in the early toddler period predicted cooperative social pretend play in the late toddler period. Cooperative social pretend play in the late toddler period predicted both sociometric ratings and teacher ratings of sociability with peers in the preschool period. These findings suggest that early social behaviors with peers predict future social competence.

The results suggest that only the constructs representing social competence in one period predict social competence in the subsequent period. Other measures of sociability with peers, such as social play, may be related to later social competence but are not independent of complementary and reciprocal and of cooperative social pretend play. The results in Chapter IV suggest that the predictive variables in the regression equations of Chapter

---

[4] Tables are available from the author on request.
[5] Tables are available from the author on request.
[6] Tables are available from the author on request.

TABLE 15

	28–45 Months	40–57 Months
Sample 1:		
16–33 months:		
Entry:		
Cooperative (easy)	.49**	.48**
Resists (rebuff)	.33*	.29
Play:		
Social	.49**	.43**
Complementary and reciprocal	.24	.21
Social pretend	.34*	.45**
Affect	.62**	.47*
28–45 months:		
Entry:		
Easy		.47**
Resist		.35*
Play:		
Social		.46*
Complementary and reciprocal		.41**
Social pretend		.52**
Cooperative social pretend		.33**
Affect		.50**
Sample 2:		
13–24 months:		
Entry:		
Easy		.62**
Rebuff		.35**
Play:		
Social		.55**
Complementary and reciprocal		.51**
Social pretend		.34**
Cooperative social pretend		.35**
Affect		.60**

		37–59 Months
25–47 months:		
Entry:		
Easy		.56**
Rebuff		.37**
Play:		
Social		.52**
Complementary and reciprocal		.37**
Social pretend		.47**
Cooperative social pretend		.28**
Affect		.52**

		60–83 Months
48–71 months:		
Entry:		
Easy		.55**
Rebuff		.43*

TABLE 15 (*Continued*)

	28–45 Months	60–83 Months
Play:		
Social		.48**
Complementary and reciprocal		.27**
Social pretend		.06
Cooperative social pretend		.21*
Affect		.61**

[a] Partial correlations with age removed.
* $p < .05$.
** $p < .01$.

V were not independent. Nevertheless, the identified behavioral constructs emerged as the best predictors within each age period.

It is important to note that both teacher ratings of children's sociability with peers and observed behavior predicted sociometric rating. Since collecting teacher ratings is more economical than obtaining observations, these findings suggest that teacher ratings of sociability might be substituted for behavioral observations. Teacher ratings also remained relatively stable over developmental periods and appear to have captured the child's orientation toward and social skill with peers.

The stability and predictiveness of individual differences in social competency with peers prior to preschool has theoretical implications. The strong connection between concurrent social behaviors and sociometric status in preschool and school age children has previously been documented (Hartup, 1983). However, studies of toddler peer interaction have been based on different conceptual notions of competency; that is, the underlying structure of the social interaction is assumed to represent more or less complex notions of the roles of self and others (Howes, 1980; Mueller & Lucas, 1975). These conceptual assumptions have not been validated with measures independent of observed social interaction. Findings of relations between toddler social skills with peers and preschool social competency with peers begins the process of validating the conceptual framework for early peer skill development.

The implications for intervention of the predictiveness of toddler social skills for future sociometric status await future research. In studies of older children, aggressive actions are associated with lower status (Coie & Kupersmidt, 1983; Dodge, 1983; Hartup, 1983). Aggressive behaviors are not captured in measures of complementary and reciprocal peer play. In fact, the following two sequences of actions, one aggressive and the other not, would receive the same rating for complementary and reciprocal peer play:

Child A hits child B and takes her toy. Child B protests and hits child A.

TABLE 16

INTERCORRELATIONS OF TEACHER RATINGS OVER TIME
IN THE LONGITUDINAL SAMPLES[a]

	28–45 Months		
	Difficult	Hesitant	Sociable
Sample 1:			
16–33 months:[b]			
Difficult	.53**	.06	−.24
Hesitant	−.28	.27	.29
Sociable	−.10	−.12	.45**
	40–57 Months		
Difficult	.45**	−.41**	−.25
Hesitant	−.74**	.33*	.16
Sociable	−.37*	−.21	.20
	40–57 Months		
28–45 months:[c]			
Difficult	.70**	−.37*	−.45**
Hesitant	−.34*	.31*	.17
Sociable	−.52**	.09	.56**
	25–36 Months		
Sample 2:			
13–24 months:[d]			
Difficult	.42**	−.11	.02
Hesitant	.06	.58**	−.30**
Sociable	−.12	−.49**	.48**
	37–59 Months		
25–47 months:[e]			
Difficult	.78**	−.08	−.36**
Hesitant	−.16	.43**	.03
Sociable	−.14	−.09	.47**
	60–83 Months		
48–71 months:[f]			
Difficult	.55**	−.33**	.04
Hesitant	.08	.28**	−.46**
Sociable	−.66**	−.12	.58**

[a] Partial correlations with age removed.
[b] $N = 42$.
[c] $N = 41$.
[d] $N = 34$.
[e] $N = 71$.
[f] $N = 118$.
* $p < .05$.
** $p < .01$.

Child A offers toy to child B. Child B receives toy, looks at it, and offers it to child A.

In the current study, social immaturity or disinterest in peers appeared to be the best marker of toddler maladaptive approachers. For example, teacher ratings of difficulty with peers were predicted by poor play skills. Future research that directly examines aggressive behaviors within the toddler period is needed to test this hypothesis.

This study differs from studies of preschool and older children in which teacher ratings of aggression are strongly associated with low sociometric ratings (Hartup, 1983). The teacher ratings of difficulty with peers used in the current study included reference to aggression with peers. However, the rating scale may not have been adequate for use with such a large age span. For example, saying no and, to some extent, biting are normative behaviors for toddler age children. Teacher ratings of toddler behaviors may not have discriminated between autonomy and aggression. At the other end of the scale, the items may not have been strong enough to discriminate between preschoolers whose overt hostility and aggression lead to peer rejection and preschoolers whose social immaturity leads to fumbled attempts to play with peers.

As predicted, the specific constructs of behaviors representing social competence within a period were not stable over developmental periods. For example, the relative proportion of complementary and reciprocal play in the early toddler period was inconsistently and modestly related to the relative proportion of complementary and reciprocal play in the late toddler period. Orientation toward peers, as represented by social play and positive affect, was stable across all developmental periods. Easy entry into peer groups remained stable across developmental periods. Entry into peer group may be a general indicator of social competence that requires different social skills at different ages. Previous research on entry behaviors has identified the components of successful entry into peer groups for preschool and older children (Dodge, 1983; Dodge et al., 1983; Putallaz, 1983; Putallaz & Gottman, 1981). Future research is needed to identify which behavioral components and strategies constitute successful entry in younger children.

The only social classification to remain stable over a 2-year period was social status. The stability of social status classifications is consistent with studies of older children (Coie & Kupersmidt, 1983; Dodge, 1983; Rubin & Daniels-Beirness, 1983). Social participation and mutual friend classifications were less stable. This suggests that orientations toward involvement with peers and establishment of friendships with peers are flexible in young children. Teachers and parents may need to take a wait-and-see attitude toward children who are liked by peers but seem to prefer solitary activities.

In sum, the behavioral constructs representing social competence in younger children predicted social competence in preschool children, as measured by both sociometric and teacher ratings. Both social behaviors and teacher ratings of peer interaction predicted future sociometric ratings.

VI. SOCIAL CLASSIFICATIONS

The goal of this chapter is to replicate and extend existing research on the social classification of preschool children. Three major topics are addressed here: (1) relations between children's social status classifications and their behaviors with peers, (2) the function of mutual friendships for children with different social status classifications, and (3) changes over time in children's behaviors with stable social classifications.

SOCIAL CLASSIFICATIONS

The observed behaviors of children with different social status and social participation classifications were compared with analysis of covariance using chronological age as a covariate. Dunn statistics were used as post hoc tests. Fifteen contrasts were used in the comparison of children with different social status classifications and six contrasts in the comparison of children with different social participation classifications. Only significant comparisons are reported.

Social Status

In general, preschool and school age children classified as rejected have a more difficult time than popular or average children entering play groups (Dodge, 1983; Dodge et al., 1983; Putallaz, 1983). I attempted to replicate this finding by comparing observed and teacher-rated behaviors of children with different social status classifications.[7] The subjects used in these comparisons were the children in the cross-sectional sample who were 3 years old and over. Children classified as rejected had fewer easy entries (M: popular = .58, rejected = .42, $tD[247] = 2.97, p < .05$) than did children classified as popular and a smaller proportion of cooperative social pretend

---

[7] Tables are available from the author on request.

play (*M:* popular = .81, rejected = .51, *tD*[247] = 2.99, *p* < .05) than did children classified as either popular or average. Children classified as rejected were rated by teachers as having more difficulty with peers than were children classified as popular (*M:* popular = 10.18, rejected = 15.44, *tD*[247] = 3.61, *p* < .01).

Social Participation

Children classified as withdrawn were expected to be less socially skilled than were children classified as active or average (Rubin, 1982). All children in the cross-sectional sample were included in the analysis of differences in observed and rated behaviors by social participation classifications.[8] Children classified as withdrawn were less likely to have easy entries (*M:* withdrawn = .36, active = .57, *tD*[326] = 3.23, *p* < .05), less likely to engage in complementary and reciprocal peer play (*M:* withdrawn = .05, active = .39, *tD*[326] = 3.24, *p* < .01) or in social pretend play (*M:* withdrawn = .15, active = .72, *tD*[326] = 3.23, *p* < .01), and less likely to show positive affect (*M:* withdrawn = .75, active = .37, *tD*[326] = 2.97, *p* < .05) than were children classified as socially active. Teachers rated socially withdrawn children as having more difficulty (*M:* withdrawn = 13.05, active = 10.73, *tD*[326] = 2.76, *p* < .05) and as being less sociable (*M:* withdrawn = 7.28, active = 9.10, *tD*[326] = 2.69, *p* < .05) than they did children classified as socially active.

THE FUNCTION OF FRIENDSHIPS

Friendship relations may be the key to entry into play groups (Corsaro, 1981). This hypothesis was explored by comparing the observed behaviors and teacher ratings of children both with and without mutual friends. A second level of analysis was used to examine the interaction between friendships and social status classifications. I asked whether a child who is rejected by classmates gains entry into play groups by virtue of friendship status. If a rejected child has a reciprocated friend, will only that friend, and generally not the other children, admit her to play groups?

Observed and Rated Behavior

The function of mutual friendships was first examined by comparing the observed and rated behaviors of children with and without mutual

[8] Tables are available from the author on request.

friends.[9] All children in the cross-sectional sample who were 3 years old and older were included in these analyses.

Mutual friend classifications were defined sociometrically. As sociometric status and mutual friend classifications were not independent, both age and sociometric rating were used as covariates in the analysis. Children with mutual friends had more easy entries (M: friends = .55, none = .34, $tD[326]$ = 3.26, $p < .01$) and engaged in more cooperative social pretend play (M: friends = .75, none = .42, $tD[326]$ = 4.15, $p < .01$) than did children with no mutual friends. Children with no mutual friends were rated by teachers as having more difficulty with peers (M: friends = 11.34, none = 14.74, $tD[326]$ = 2.91, $p < .05$) and as being less sociable with peers (M: friends = 9.42, none = 7.87, $tD[326]$ = 2.94, $p < .05$) than were children with mutual friends.

Entry

Entry attempts with friends versus acquaintances were compared for children with different social status classifications. This allowed for a further examination of the relations between social status classification and entry behavior. Only children with reciprocal friends were included in this analysis. The comparisons were computed separately for easy and for rebuffed entry attempts. Analysis of covariance using chronological age as a covariate and Dunn statistics with 15 contrasts were used to make the comparisons.[10] Only significant comparisons are reported. Children classified as rejected were more likely to have easy entries with friends than with acquaintances (M: friends = 8.97, acquaintances = 1.69, $tD[216]$ = 4.27, $p < .01$). Children classified as popular or average were more likely to have easy entries with acquaintances than with friends (M: popular, friends = 4.16, acquaintances = 7.24; average, friends = 1.14, acquaintances = 4.27, $tD[216]$ = 2.98, $p < .05$). In general, children tended to enter groups composed of acquaintances rather than friends (M: number of entries with friends = 2.56, number of entries with acquaintances = 8.52). Therefore, it is not surprising that children classified as popular and average had more easy entries with acquaintances than with friends. Children classified as popular had easy entries 91% of the time they attempted entry with friends and 70% of the time they attempted entry with acquaintances. In contrast, children classified as rejected had easy entries 82% of the time they attempted entry with friends but only 16% of the time they attempted entry with acquaintances.

[9] Tables are available from the author on request.
[10] Tables are available from the author on request.

Children of all social status classifications were more likely to be rebuffed by acquaintances than by friends (*M:* popular, friends = .41, acquaintances = 3.14, $tD[216]$ = 3.05, $p < .05$; controversial, friends = 3.97, acquaintances = 6.01, $tD[216]$ = 3.09, $p < .05$; rejected, friends = 2.01, acquaintances = 9.13, $tD[216]$ = 3.17, $p < .05$; average, friends = 2.73, acquaintances = 4.14, $tD[216]$ = 3.15, $p < .05$).

CHANGES IN THE BEHAVIOR OF CHILDREN
WITH STABLE SOCIAL STATUS CLASSIFICATION

The question of change in behaviors and ratings of children with stable social status and social participation classifications was examined. The combined longitudinal samples were used to examine changes in observed and rated behaviors in preschool age children with stable social status classifications. Analysis of covariance using chronological age as a covariate and Dunn statistics with 15 contrasts were used to make the comparisons.[11] Only significant comparisons are reported. Children with stable rejected classifications (N = 15) decreased their proportion of easy entries (time 1: M = .55; time 2: M = .31, $tD[127]$ = 3.09, $p < .05$), increased their proportion of rebuffed entries (time 1: M = .39; time 2: M = .47, $tD[127]$ = 2.97, $p < .05$), and decreased their proportion of positive affect (time 1: M = .88; time 2: M = .46, $tD[127]$ = 3.14, $p < .05$) over time.

In order to examine Rubin's (Rubin et al., in press) hypothesis that early social withdrawal is associated with eventual peer rejection, the association between social withdrawal and rejected sociometric status 1 year later was examined in longitudinal sample 2. There was a significant association, $\chi^2(4)$ = 22.03, $p < .05$. Sixty percent of those children classified as socially withdrawn were classified as sociometrically rejected 1 year later, 20% as neglected, and 20% as average. There were no age differences in this association.

SUMMARY AND DISCUSSION

The results are consistent with previous research on associations between sociometric status and social behaviors. Children with rejected classifications were more likely to be rebuffed by their peers and were described by their teachers as having difficulty with peers. However, for older rejected children (e.g., Dodge, 1983), aversive behavior is the most important behavior associated with rejected status. The current study did not

[11] Tables are available from the author on request.

observe maladaptive behaviors. Therefore, although the children with rejected social status in the current study were rejected by their peers when they attempted to enter play groups, we do not know if their behavior was aggressive or aversive or if their play group entries were inept.

This study is one of the first to examine changes in behavior of children with stable social status classifications. It is interesting that the rejected children became both less successful in their play group entries and less positive in their affect with peers over time. This suggests both that the rejected children's behavior became more aversive and that their peers were less willing to accommodate and engage with them.

Children in the current study who were classified as less socially active engaged in less complex play interactions with peers than did children classified as socially active. This finding is consistent with Rubin's (1982) report that socially withdrawn kindergartners engaged in less mature play forms than did their peers, even though the definition of social withdrawal in this study is less stringent than Rubin's definition. As social participation was a relatively unstable social classification (see Chap. V), an analysis of changes in observed behaviors and ratings in children with stable social participation classifications could not be completed. However, Rubin et al. (in press) have suggested that some proportion of older withdrawn children eventually are rejected by their peers. This hypothesis was partially supported when I tested it with younger children. Slightly over half the socially withdrawn children were classified as rejected in a subsequent year.

The function and significance of reciprocal friendships is highlighted by the analyses presented in this chapter. Children with no mutual friends had a harder time entering play groups, engaged in less skillful interaction, and received lower teacher ratings than did children with friends. Children classified as rejected were more likely to have easy entries with friends than with acquaintances. They were less likely to be rebuffed by friends than by acquaintances when they attempted to enter a play group. These findings suggest that a reciprocated friend may facilitate experiences of entering play for children who are less competent in peer interaction. The implications of such findings include expanding intervention programs for at-risk children to include friendship-making opportunities as well as social skill training.

Children with sociometric and social participation classifications similar to those reported in the literature for older children showed similar patterns of behavior. Children classified as rejected were rebuffed by their peers, and children classified as withdrawn were less socially mature. Socially withdrawn children tended to become classified as rejected rather than neglected. Children in at-risk classifications who had reciprocated friendships had greater access to play groups and spent more time in social pretend play than did those at-risk children without reciprocated friendships.

VII. INFLUENCES OF VARIATIONS IN EXPERIENCE WITH PEERS

⌈I expected children with more social experience with peers to be more socially competent.⌉I examined several kinds of social experience: the amount of time the child had spent with the peers with whom she was observed; her experience with siblings; and the amount of time the child had spent in daily intimate associations with agemates. Experience with the peers with whom the child was observed and experience with siblings constituted experience with particular peers. Experiences with agemates constituted experience with peers in general.

EXPERIENCE WITH PARTICULAR PEERS

Children were classified as having had more time in their peer group if they had been in the same peer group for a year or more and as having less time in their peer group if they had entered it between 6 and 12 months before the observations. Children were classified as having experience with siblings if they had a sibling within 3 years of their own age.

⌊I examined the influence of experiences with particular peers with 2 × 2 analyses of covariance for time in group (less than 12 vs. 12 or more months) and sibling status (yes, no) with chronological age as a covariate done separately for three age groups (early toddler, late toddler, and preschool). Dependent variables were observed and rated behaviors. To decrease the number of comparisons and to provide conceptual clarity, the number of age groups was reduced to three: early toddler (1-year-olds), late toddler (2- and 3-year-olds), and preschool (4–6-year-olds). Twenty-one Dunn statistics post hoc contrasts were made. Only significant comparisons are reported.

Comparisons of observed behaviors and ratings for children in each of the three age groups (early toddler, late toddler, and preschool) for children who had spent a year or more in the peer group versus less than a year are presented in Table 17. Children in the early toddler period who spent more time in their peer group engaged in more complementary and reciprocal peer play, $tD(28) = 3.75$, $p < .05$, and were rated by teachers as having less difficulty with peers, $tD(28) = 3.65$, $p < .05$, than were children who had spent less time in the peer group. Children in the late toddler period who had spent more time in their peer group engaged in more cooperative social pretend play, $tD(37) = 3.34$, $p < .05$, and were rated by teachers as having less difficulty with peers, $tD(37) = 3.74$, $p < .05$, than were children who had spent less time in the peer group. Children in the preschool period who had spent more time in their peer group had higher sociometric ratings, $tD(190) = 3.47$, $p < .05$, than were children who had spent less time in their peer group.

EXPERIENCE WITH PEERS IN GENERAL

Experience with peers in general was represented by the age the child entered child care. Children were classified into five groups: entering child care at 12 months of age or less, entering between 13 and 24 months, entering between 25 and 36 months, entering between 37 and 48 months, and entering after 48 months.

The number of months a child was in a particular peer group was confounded with the age the child entered child care and the age at observation (if a toddler and preschooler both entered child care as infants and remained in a single child care arrangement, the toddler would be scored as having less time in the group). Therefore, I analyzed experiences with peers in general separately for each age group described earlier. Within each age group, one-way analyses of covariance tests using chronological age as a covariate were conducted with either two (early toddler group), three (late toddler group), or five (preschool group) comparison groups.[12] Six contrasts using Dunn statistics were made in the late toddler comparisons. Fifteen contrasts were made in the preschool comparisons. Only significant comparisons are reported.

Children in the early toddler period who entered child care as 1-year-olds were rated by teachers as having more difficulty with peers than did children who entered as infants (age ≤ 12 months: $M = 12.90$; age = 13–24 months: $M = 17.14$, $tD[33] = 3.20$, $p < .05$). Children in the late toddler period who entered child care when they were 2 years old or older engaged

---

[12] Tables are available from the author on request.

TABLE 17

COMPARISON OF OBSERVED BEHAVIORS AND RATINGS AS A FUNCTION OF TIME
IN THE PEER GROUP

| | TIME IN THE GROUP | | | |
| | Less | | More | |
OBSERVED BEHAVIORS AND RATINGS	M	SD	M	SD
Early toddler:[a]				
Entry:				
Easy	.32	.24	.40	.15
Rebuff	.38	.14	.32	.22
Play:				
Social	.66	.54	.59	.47
Complementary and reciprocal	.02	.01	.08	.06
Social pretend	.19	.17	.35	.26
Cooperative	.06	.05	.04	.01
Affect	.58	.13	.68	.42
Teacher ratings:				
Difficult	14.83	9.74	12.00	8.16
Hesitant	11.61	8.14	11.60	7.36
Sociable	7.28	7.15	6.81	6.13
Late toddler:[b]				
Entry:				
Easy	.46	.36	.47	.41
Rebuff	.39	.21	.23	.14
Play:				
Social	.73	.56	.78	.71
Complementary and reciprocal	.15	.12	.20	.15
Social pretend	.39	.26	.52	.31
Cooperative	.27	.16	.71	.13
Affect	.76	.54	.73	.12
Teacher ratings:				
Difficult	14.27	9.86	11.48	9.17
Hesitant	9.76	6.84	10.89	9.13
Sociable	9.41	8.14	8.22	7.73
Preschool:[c]				
Entry:				
Easy	.54	.32	.50	.47
Rebuff	.19	.12	.22	.16
Play:				
Social	.80	.71	.73	.62
Complementary and reciprocal	.40	.23	.44	.31
Social pretend	.73	.54	.78	.32
Cooperative	.81	.57	.89	.63
Affect	.77	.35	.88	.52
Teacher ratings:				
Difficult	15.04	1.35	12.53	2.97
Hesitant	8.29	2.44	8.41	1.96
Sociable	9.15	4.08	11.01	3.26
Sociometric ratings	−.57	.08	.62	.37

[a] 13–24 months.
[b] 2–3 years.
[c] 4–6 years.

in less cooperative social pretend play than did children who entered child care before their second birthdays (age ≤ 24 months: M = .86; age = 25–36 months: M = .60, $tD[40]$ = 3.21, p < .05). Children in the preschool period who entered child care when they were 2 years old or older experienced more rebuffed entries (age ≤ 24 months: M = .08; age > 24 months: M = .28, $tD[193]$ = 3.25, p < .05) than did children who entered earlier. Children in the preschool period who entered child care when they were 3 years old or older engaged in less cooperative social pretend play (age ≥ 37 months: M = .41; age ≤ 36 months: M = .86, $tD[193]$ = 3.31, p < .05), had lower sociometric ratings (age ≥ 37 months: M = −.46; age ≤ 36 months: M = .36, $tD[193]$ = 3.27, p < .05), and were rated by teachers as having more difficulty with peers (age ≥ 37 months: M = 15.23; age ≥ 36 months: M = 13.01, $tD[193]$ = 3.45, p < .05) than were children who entered earlier.

PEER EXPERIENCES OF CHILDREN WITH DIFFERENT SOCIAL CLASSIFICATIONS

I examined the influence of experiences with peers for social classifications by comparing the age of entry into child care for preschool children with different classifications. These comparisons were done twice: once with the cross-sectional sample and once with the combined longitudinal samples using only those children with stable classifications. Analyses of covariance, using chronological age as a covariate and Dunn statistics, were used to compare children with different classifications.[13] Fifteen contrasts were made to compare children with different social status classifications. Six contrasts were made to compare children with different social participation and to compare children with different mutual friend classifications. Only significant comparisons are reported.

Cross-sectional Sample

Children who were classified as popular or average in social status entered child care at earlier ages than did children classified as rejected (M age of entry: popular = 10.5 months, average = 11.0 months, rejected = 30.9 months, $tD[247]$ = 3.27, p < .05). Children with no mutual friends similarly entered child care later than did children with many friends (M age of entry: no friends = 37.2 months, friends = 16.6 months, $tD[326]$ = 3.34, p < .01). Children with different social participation classifications were not different in their age of entry.

---

[13] Tables are available from the author on request.

Longitudinal Sample

Children with stable popular or average status classifications entered child care earlier than did children with stable rejected classifications (age entered: popular = 18.9 months, average = 14.2 months, rejected = 33.0 months, $tD[25]$ = 3.51, p < .05). Children with stable no mutual friends classifications entered child care later (age entered: no friends = 48.7, friends = 5.0, $tD[33]$ = 3.63, p < .05) than did children with stable friend classifications. Children with stable different social participation classifications were no different in early peer experience.

CHILDREN WHO MOVED

Between years 1 and 2, 23 children in longitudinal sample 1 moved between child care centers and/or peer groups. There were no differences in year 1 measures of observed behaviors between those who later did or did not move. Differences in observed behaviors in year 2 between children in longitudinal sample 1 who moved between child care centers with a portion of their previous peer group (N = 18) were compared with those who moved between child care centers and changed peer groups (N = 7) and those who remained in the same child care center and peer group (N = 18). No children changed peer groups within a center. One-way analyses of covariance using chronological age as a covariate and Dunn statistics with six contrasts were used to compare these three groups.[14] Only significant comparisons are reported. Children who moved with members of their peer group to a different child care center had higher proportions of complementary and reciprocal peer play (moved with group: M = .45; other: M = .26, $tD[38]$ = 3.01, p < .05) than did children who stayed in the same child care center with the same peer group or who moved alone.

Children who stayed in the same peer group and child care center or who moved to a different child care center with members of their peer group were rated by teachers as more sociable than were children who moved alone (moved alone: M = 8.17; moved with peer group: M = 11.14, $tD[38]$ = 2.97, p < .05).

Between years 2 and 3, 105 children in the combined longitudinal samples moved between peer groups within the same child care center, nine children moved to a different child care center with members of their peer group, 15 moved to different child care centers with different peer groups, and 125 children remained with their peer group. Because the same obser-

---

[14] Tables are available from the author on request.

vational measures were used in years 2 and 3, changes in observed and rated behaviors could be examined. Change scores were calculated by converting observation and rating scores into standard scores calculated within each age group and subtracting standard scores from year 2 from standard scores from year 3. One-way analyses of covariance, using chronological age as a covariate, and Dunn statistics with 10 contrasts were used to compare groups.[15] Only significant comparisons are reported.

Children who stayed in the same child care center with the same peer group increased their proportion of complementary and reciprocal peer play, $tD(144) = 3.20$, $p < .05$, more than did children who stayed in the same child care center but changed peer groups. Children who moved to a new child care center with a portion of their peer group increased their proportion of complementary and reciprocal peer play more than did children who changed child care centers without members of their peer group, $tD(144) = 3.20$, $p < .05$.

SUMMARY AND DISCUSSION

The current chapter examined associations between individual differences in social experiences with peers and social competence with peers. The findings suggest that, for toddlers, experience with particular peers in stable peer groups facilitates the mastery of social interaction skills. Toddlers who spent a year or more with the same peers engaged in more competent social interaction with peers and were rated as having less difficulty with peers than were children who had been in the peer group less than a year. The presymbolic nature of toddler peer interaction appears to be dependent on peer familiarity (Mueller & Vandell, 1979). The findings of the current study suggest that, for toddlers, peer familiarity requires many months of sustained contact. Preschool children who had more experience with particular peers were not more socially skilled than their peers who entered the peer group later. The differences in findings between toddler and preschool age children may reflect differences in the social skills used in peer interaction at different ages. Toddlers are more dependent on idiosyncratic routines for play than are preschoolers, whose mastery of spoken or signed language permits more general communication and play. However, the preschool children in this study received higher sociometric ratings if they had more experience with particular peers. This suggests that experience with particular peers also may contribute to the development of social skills in older children.

Children who moved had less experience with particular peers than

[15] Tables are available from the author on request.

children who stayed in the same peer groups between study years. In general, it appears that children who move, particularly those who move without familiar peers, may be less socially competent than children who remain. Therefore, as with adults, the experience of moving may be difficult for children and contribute to less mature forms of play with peers.

Alternately, children who move may differ from those who do not in characteristics not assessed in the current study but important in the development of social competence with peers. For example, a child may be moved because the parents are divorcing, because a parent lost her job, because the parents failed to pay tuition, or because the parents were in conflict with the child care center. Any of these reasons may create stress for the child and interfere with relations with peers. Furthermore, within a child care center, the child could move from being the oldest in the group to being the youngest. This experience could induce qualitative changes in social behaviors (French, in press).

Children who moved between peer groups with peers, as opposed to moving to a new peer group without peers, appeared to have less difficulty with moving. The pattern of results in the current study suggests that children who move with peers may use their peers for emotional support. Teachers rated these children as more sociable than children who moved alone. Children who moved with peers increased their proportion of complementary and reciprocal play during the next year. Children who moved alone did not increase in social competence during the year following the move. The presence of familiar peers in an otherwise strange setting may orient the children toward the peer group and focus their development of social skills.

However, parents of children who move with peers may differ in the value placed on social relationships from parents of children who move alone. One group of seven children in longitudinal sample 1 moved to new child care centers as a group twice, between study years 1 and 2 and again between study years 2 and 3. During the sociometric interview in year 3 of the study, one of the children told the examiner, "Of course, these children are all my friends. They've always been my friends." This particular group of children was very stable because the parents all had become friends during their children's enrollment in the first child care center. The parents valued peer friendships and made adjustments in their own lives (e.g., carpools and inconvenient location of the child care center) to maintain their adult friendships and to keep the children together. Parents' own social networks are important in the friendship formation and social skills of their children (Espinosa & Howes, 1984; Rubin & Sloman, 1984). It appears that the value the parents placed on relationships with peers may have enhanced the social competence of this particular sample of children.

Children who had more experience with peers in general also appeared more socially competent with peers. Although no single measure of social competence with peers was significant across any two of the three age groups, differences in social competence within each age group were consistent with the pattern of behavioral constructs representing social competence within each period. Children observed during the late toddler period engaged in more social pretend play if they were in the early entry group. Children observed during the preschool period had higher sociometric ratings if they were in the early entry group.

The analyses of the social experiences of children with different social classifications were consistent with the previous analyses. Children in the cross-sectional sample who were classified as rejected and children in the longitudinal sample who had stable rejected classifications entered peer groups at older ages than did children with other classifications. This finding may be particular to the context of the current study. The child care groups observed in the study tended to have at least a core group of well-acquainted children. Some of these children had been together for 6–10 hours a day for 3–4 years. A new child entering the group, particularly one who had little experience with other peers, may have been treated as an intruder by the more established group.

The differences in the current study between children who entered child care as infants, toddlers, or preschoolers suggest that a benefit of early entry into child care may be increased social competence with peers. No measures of individual differences in children's cognitive competence or social relations with adults were included in this study. Children who entered child care at an older age may have done so because their parents judged them to be developmentally immature or inhibited in their social relations. These characteristics would have interfered with establishing relationships with peers. Parents who place their children in child care as infants also may differ from parents who do so later. Parents of early entering children may place less value on exclusive adult-child relationships and more on children's relationships with a wider social network.

Children classified as socially withdrawn, again using a less stringent definition than Rubin, did not differ from children classified as average or active in social experience with peers. This finding supports Rubin's hypothesis (Rubin & Lollis, 1988) that the antecedents of social withdrawal lie outside the peer system, in the sphere of parental attachments or in behavioral inhibition.

Experiences with siblings, in the current study, did not influence the social behavior of children with peers. The children in the study were with peers more hours per day than they were with their siblings. Thus, sibling experiences may have had little effect on social skills. When siblings are the primary peer contact for the child, as they are in traditional families, they may have more influence on the development of social competency with peers (Pepler, Corter, & Abramovitch, 1982).

In sum, the current study found associations between individual differences in behaviors with peers and variations in time with peers in general and in time with particular peers but not in experience with siblings.

VIII. THE STABILITY OF EARLY FRIENDSHIPS

KEEPING FRIENDS

I tested the hypothesis that child care children form stable friendships fairly early in their lives and that these friendships remain as a constant part of the child's social network. I examined the stability of friendships in the portion of the current sample that remained in stable peer groups. All dyads that remained in the same peer groups for either 2 or 3 years ($N = 2,576$) were classified as reciprocal (both nominated the other), unilateral (only one pair in the dyad was nominated), or as not friends (received no nominations). In study year 1, children were classified as friends or not friends on the basis of teacher nominations. In study years 2 and 3, only sociometrically identified friendships were used in the analysis. The percent of dyads that maintained and changed friendship classifications in each group is presented in Table 18. Children tended to maintain their relationships over a 2-year, but not a 3-year, period. There were no differences by age of child.

Seventy-six percent of the children who stayed in the same peer group as their reciprocated friend but did not maintain a reciprocal friendship over time formed at least one new reciprocated friendship in the subsequent year. There were no age differences in the likelihood of replacing a lost friend, $\chi^2(1) = 1.42$, N.S. Fifty-three percent of those children who did not remain in the same peer group as their reciprocated friend over time formed at least one new reciprocated friendship with another child in the subsequent year. Again, there were no age differences in the likelihood of replacing a lost friend, $\chi^2(1) = 2.43$, N.S.

SEPARATION FROM FRIENDS

The majority of the children in the two longitudinal samples experienced losing a friend. Children lost friends both because their parents changed their child care settings and because within the schools the peer

61

TABLE 18

STABILITY OF FRIENDSHIPS OVER TIME IN THE LONGITUDINAL SAMPLES[a]

	28–45 MONTHS			
	Not Friends	Unilateral	Reciprocal	χ^2
Longitudinal sample 1:				
16–33 months:				
Not friends	77	18	5	12.22*
Friends	21	28	51	
	40–57 MONTHS			
Not friends	80	13	7	
Friends	29	61	10	3.23
	25–36 MONTHS			
Combined longitudinal samples:				
13–24 months:				
Not friends	90	8	2	
Unilateral friends	71	21	8	
Reciprocal friends	10	21	69	12.67*
	3 AND 4 YEARS			
2 and 3 years:				
Not friends	94	5	1	
Unilateral friends	67	23	10	
Reciprocal friends	5	31	65	11.74*
	5 AND 6 YEARS			
4 and 5 years:				
Not friends	97	3	0	
Unilateral friends	46	39	15	
Reciprocal friends	3	27	70	13.63*

[a] Percent of dyads that changed or maintained their classification is reported. Chi-square analyses were conducted on actual frequencies.
* $p < .05$.

group composition changed. The modal experience for the children in the sample was to lose a friend because the friend left, to end a friendship even though the friend remained in the school, and to keep a friendship. I examined the influence of the loss of reciprocal friends on social competence with peers by computing the proportion of mutual friendships kept, ended, or lost for each child who remained in the same peer group between years of the study. Children were not classified because the categories were not mutually exclusive.

Children in longitudinal sample 1 were given scores for percent of reciprocated friendships (identified by sociometrics in years 2 and 3 and by teachers in year 1) kept, lost, and ended over a 1- and 2-year period. Children in longitudinal sample 2 were given scores for percent of sociometric reciprocated friendships kept, lost, and ended over a 1-year period. I then correlated the percent of friendships kept, lost, and ended with observed and rated behaviors. These Pearson product-moment correlations are presented in Table 19.

Children in longitudinal sample 1 who kept a higher percent of their friendships between the ages of 16–33 and 28–45 months engaged in more easy entry, social pretend play, and cooperative social pretend play. They also had higher sociometric ratings in the second year. The children in the combined longitudinal samples who kept a higher percent of their friendships over a 1-year period engaged in more easy entry, social play, complementary and reciprocal peer play, social pretend play, and cooperative social pretend play. They also had higher sociometric ratings and teacher ratings of sociability.

Children in longitudinal sample 1 who kept a higher percent of their friendships over a 2-year period had higher complementary and reciprocal peer play, cooperative social pretend scores, and sociometric ratings and had ratings of less difficulty with peers.

Children in longitudinal sample 1 who ended a higher percent of friendships between the ages of 16–33 and 28–45 months were rated by the teacher as having greater difficulty and being less hesitant and less sociable with peers in the subsequent year. Children in the combined longitudinal samples who ended a higher percent of friendships had higher scores for rebuffed entries and lower sociometric ratings in the subsequent year.

Children in longitudinal sample 1 who lost a high percent of friendships between the ages of 16–33 and 28–45 months had higher easy entry scores but lower cooperative social pretend scores and lower teacher ratings of difficulty with peers. Children in the combined longitudinal samples who lost a high percent of friendships had low rebuff entry scores and high social play scores but had lower cooperative social pretend play scores and sociometric ratings. Teachers rated them as more hesitant with peers in the subsequent year.

SUMMARY AND DISCUSSION

Children tended to maintain their reciprocal friendships if they could. The particular nature of the sample may have contributed to the stability of the friendships. All the children were enrolled full time in child care. Many of them were enrolled since they were infants and toddlers. This particular population of children may be both more aware of and more dependent on their peer group than are non–child care children. Parents and teachers

TABLE 19

RELATIONS BETWEEN OBSERVED SOCIAL BEHAVIORS AND SOCIOMETRIC RATINGS WHEN FRIENDS WERE KEPT OR LOST

	LONGITUDINAL SAMPLE 1			
OBSERVED BEHAVIOR	Friendships Kept for 1 Year (%)	Friendships Ended (%)	Friendships Lost by Moving (%)	Friendships Kept for 2 Years (%)
Entry:				
Easy	.26*	−.06	.25*	...
Rebuff	.01	.09	−.13	...
Play:				
Social	.03	−.16	.13	...
Complementary and reciprocal	.01	−.08	.14	...
Social pretend	.38**	−.17	−.21	...
Cooperative	.44**	.18	−.27*	...
Affect	.01	.07	.03	...
Sociometric rating	.25*	.02	.16	...
Teacher rating:				
Difficult	.02	.48**	−.44***	...
Hesitant	−.05	−.26*	.20	...
Social	.21	−.31**	.17	...

	Combined Longitudinal Samples			Longitudinal Sample 1
Entry:				
Easy	.30**	.03	.04	.18
Rebuff	.04	.18*	−.19*	−.13
Play:				
Social	.30**	.03	.25*	.10
Complimentary and reciprocal	.58**	.02	.10	.35*
Social pretend	.67***	.02	.09	.26
Cooperative	.51**	.04	−.23*	.51**
Affect	.05	.10	−.15	.06
Sociometric rating	.51**	−.18*	−.22*	.40**
Teacher rating:				
Difficult	−.01	.07	.03	−.41**
Hesitant	−.05	−.13	.25*	.03
Sociability	.25*	.06	.02	.13

* $p \leq .05$.
** $p \leq .01$.

65

also may have contributed to the stability of these friendships by encouraging children who initially formed friendships to maintain them by such activities as labeling the children as friends and promoting visiting outside of class.

The children's friendships in this study were fluid as well as stable. While some friendship relationships were maintained for as long as 3 years, most of the children also had experiences making new friends, separating from old friends, and ending friendships. Most of the children who lost friends through separation replaced them with other reciprocal friends. This finding suggests that children with the skills to form one friendship can form another.

Children whose friendships ended even though the old friend was available in the peer group were more likely to replace the friend than were children who lost a friend because the old friend moved. This finding is unexpected as social skills are at least as important to keeping friendships as to initiating friendships. Howes (1983) and Lederberg et al. (1987) report that preschoolers form both temporary and stable friendships. The design of the current study did not permit classifying the friendships of each year as either temporary or stable. The replacement friendships of the children whose friendship ended even though the old friend was available in the peer group may have been temporary rather than stable.

Friendships outside the classroom were not assessed in this study. Therefore, it is possible that some of the old friendships with children who left the peer group still existed and were maintained by contacts facilitated by parents. Children who had such friendships outside child care may have felt less need to form new friendship relationships inside child care.

Elsewhere, I have suggested (Howes, 1983) that peer friendships take on emotional significance to the child not dissimilar in form, though dissimilar in intensity and developmental significance, to the parent attachment. The findings of the current study regarding the experiences of children who lost and maintained friendships are consistent with the notion of early friendships as peer attachments. Children who lost a high proportion of friends because the friends moved and children who moved to new peer groups without familiar peers were less socially skilled than were children who stayed with friends. In contrast, keeping a high proportion of toddler friendships through preschool was associated with high levels of social skills and with higher sociometric ratings.

Losing friends appears to have some long-term effects on children. If children exhibit distress at separation from friends, then the type of friendships formed in child care are not the transitory relationships described in studies of the social cognition of friendship (Selman, Jaquette, & Lavin, 1977). Furthermore, if the stability of the peer group is associated with the development of social competency with peers, then parents and teachers may need to be more sensitive to the issue of maintaining friendships.

In summary, between 50% and 70% of the reciprocated friendships identified in this study were maintained from one year to the next. Ten percent of the friendships formed in the toddler period were maintained for 2 years. This degree of stability in friendships is greater than predicted from the previous literature on preschool friendships. The stability of the friendships in this sample suggests that children who have sustained intimate experiences with the same peers may receive emotional support from them. Children who maintained a large proportion of their friendships appeared to be more socially competent than children who lost their friends through separation. This suggests that, in these young children, some social skills may be particular to dyadic relationships. In the absence of the relationship, the child may appear less socially skilled.

IX. CONCLUSIONS

SEQUENCES AND INDIVIDUAL DIFFERENCES IN SOCIAL SKILLS

The predicted sequence of behavioral constructs representing social competence with peers was supported. Complementary and reciprocal play in the early toddler period and cooperative social pretend play in the late toddler period increased proportionally when examined cross sectionally and longitudinally. There was no adequate test in the current study of the proposed sequence from late toddler to preschool. Future research needs to include assessments of social cognition as well as observations and ratings of social competence to test the existence of such a sequence.

The assumption that the identified behavioral constructs within each period represent individual differences in social competence with peers was also supported by the results of the study. Individual differences in the proportion of complementary and reciprocal play in the early toddler period, in the proportion of cooperative social pretend play in the late toddler period, and in sociometric status in the preschool period were associated with individual differences in the ease that the child entered play groups and in teacher ratings of social competence.

The predicted stability of measures of social competence across developmental periods also was supported. The behavioral constructs representing social competence in the early toddler period (complementary and reciprocal peer play) predicted the behavioral construct representing social competence in the late toddler period (cooperative social pretend play). The behavioral construct representing social competence in the late toddler period (cooperative social pretend play) predicted sociometric status and teacher ratings of social competence in preschool.

Teacher and sociometric ratings with peers appeared to be viable assessment alternatives for preschool social competence with peers. Teacher assessments may be a more reliable alternative when assessments are made on children who are enrolled in less stable peer groups than were the children assessed in the current study. Future researchers might consider using different items on teacher rating scales for toddlers than for preschoolers.

Despite the support for the predictive power of individual differences in toddler behaviors with peers for preschool social competence, the amount of variance explained by such individual differences never exceeded 50%. Other sources of individual differences in preschool social competence with peers include individual differences in attachment relationships with caregiving adults (Sroufe, 1981, 1983), in socialization experiences (Parke, Mac-Donald, Beitel, & Bhanager, 1986), in cognitive and linguistic competence (Brownell, 1986), and in experiences with peers outside formal child care settings. Furthermore, individual differences in the child's attachment relationships or socialization experiences with primary caregivers may underlie individual differences in toddler behavior with peers (Sroufe, 1981).

The toddler period does not appear to function as a necessary or critical period for the development of peer interaction skills. All the preschool children observed in the current study engaged in complementary and reciprocal peer play and cooperative social pretend play regardless of when they began daily experience with peers. The constructs of competent interaction with peers suggested by the current study do provide tools for assessing early peer interaction. Future research is needed to explore the concurrent correlates of successful and unsuccessful peer interaction in the toddler period.

Individual differences in children's social experiences with peers, with both particular peers and peers in general, related to individual differences in observed and rated behaviors with peers. These findings have a practical application. It appears that early child care, particularly if the child is in a stable peer group, can be beneficial for social development. Children who enter child care earlier appear to have an easier time with peers as preschoolers. This finding is in sharp contrast to Belsky's (in press) suggestion that infant child care places children at risk for later social development. Other factors may account for this relation. Self-selection is the most likely alternative explanation. It is possible that parents who believed their children would have a difficult time with peers do not enter them in child care until preschool age. It is possible that parents who enroll their children as infants differ in their value systems and child-rearing practices from those who enroll their children as preschoolers.

DEFINITION OF CONSTRUCTS

One of the goals of the current study was to identify the behavioral constructs that represent competent behavior with peers within the developmental period. Multiple methods—observations, teacher ratings, and sociometric interviews—were used to assess social competence with peers. Observations of play behaviors may be a more sophisticated method than observations of rates of social participation or of rates of positive versus aggressive acts for assessing early competence (Asher, Markell, & Hymel, 1981). This is not the first study to assess such behavior. Complementary and reciprocal peer play is similar to forms of early peer interaction studied by Eckerman (Eckerman & Stein, 1982; Eckerman, Whatley, & Kutz, 1975), Goldman (Goldman & Ross, 1978), and Ross (1982; Ross, Lollois, & Elliott, 1982). Rubin's assessment of peer interaction is only one of a number of schemes used to classifying structure and content in preschool children (Rubin & Daniels-Beirness, 1983).

This is one of the first studies to explore extensively the reliability and validity of complex observational measures of peer interaction using both teacher and peer ratings as alternative assessments. Measures of children's play interactions during the two toddler periods substantially agreed with teacher ratings of competence in peer interaction.

The measure of cooperative social pretend play used in the current study, although related to teacher and peer assessments of competence, did not capture the full complexity of social pretend play in the preschool period. Future research in this area might adopt more complex measures of fantasy play that include assessments of the use of meta-communications and the type and range of roles (e.g., leader or victims) assumed in the play (Connolly & Doyle, 1984; Rosenberg, 1985).

Teacher ratings of competence with peers were related to concurrent measures of interaction with peers and were predictive of preschool sociometric ratings. Teacher ratings of sociability with peers were more useful than were teacher ratings of difficulty and hesitancy with peers. The limited usefulness of teacher ratings of difficulty and hesitancy with peers may be related to our limited knowledge of the behavioral manifestations of problematic interaction with peers in younger children. For example, it is developmentally appropriate for toddlers to experience difficulty in sharing. There are no assessments to determine when a toddler's difficulty in sharing moves from the normative to the problematic. Future research is needed to identify the parameters of difficulty and hesitancy with peers in the toddler period.

Higher than expected test-retest reliability of sociometric nominations was found in this study. This is contrary to the expectations derived from the literature on preschool children's sociometric nominations (Hymel, 1983). The test-retest reliability of the sociometric nominations appears related to the particular social circumstances of the children in the study and should not be used as an indication of the general utility of sociometric nominations in preschool children. The success of the rating sociometric status classification system used in the current study is promising. If ratings can be used to define social status classifications, they can be used with preschool children who have a range of experiences with peers. Future research is needed to replicate the utility of the alternative system for preschool age children.

Sociometric nominations may be more useful for identifying mutual friends in preschoolers than they are for assessing social status. Sociometric nominations substantially agreed with teacher and behavioral identification of reciprocated friendships. Mutual friend classifications, based on sociometric nominations, differentiated between children of greater and lesser social skills. Children classified as rejected had few mutually nominated friends, while those classified as popular had many.

The method of behaviorally identifying friendships in the current study was designed to accommodate the presymbolic nature of toddler age children but was used for children of all ages. Therefore, the behavioral identification measure of friendships may not have been subtle enough to capture the nuances of preschool age friendships. Future research may be needed to redesign this measure for preschoolers.

SOCIAL CLASSIFICATION OF CHILDREN

Social status classifications remained relatively stable over a year in preschool. The level of stability of status was consistent with reports of stability of status in older children (Coie & Dodge, 1983; Rubin & Daniels-Beirness, 1983). Children with different social status classifications behaved differently. These results are consistent with previous research on sociometric classifications (Hartup, 1983).

The findings on social participation classifications in the current study, although based on less stringent criteria than those used by Rubin (1982), also were similar to those found in previous research (Rubin, 1982, 1985). Social participation classifications were relatively unstable but were related to observed social play. Children classified as withdrawn tended to engage in less complex play with peers.

The current study also supports the hypothesis that social withdrawal and sociometric neglect are independent (Rubin, 1982, 1985; Rubin et al., in press). There was little agreement between classification systems. Children classified as socially withdrawn were more likely to be classified as rejected than as neglected in a subsequent year. These findings need further replication as the social status classification system used does not reliably identify neglected children (Asher & Dodge, 1986).

The exploration of social experiences with peers also supports the independence of social status and social participation classifications. Children classified as rejected by peers generally had less experience with peers than did children classified as popular. However, children classified as socially withdrawn were similar in peer experience to children classified as socially active. Socially withdrawn children may have problematic attachment relationships with care givers or be socially inhibited. They do appear to have had similar amounts of experiences with peers as children classified as socially active. These findings support the hypothesis proposed by Rubin (Rubin & Lollis, 1988) that the origins of social withdrawal lie outside the peer system.

FRIENDSHIPS

The current study highlighted the importance of mutual friends for young children. Children who kept a larger proportion of reciprocal friends over a 1-year period were more socially competent than were those who lost their reciprocal friends. Mutual friends lessen peer rejection, particularly for entry into play groups. Mutual friends also facilitate the acquisition of developmentally appropriate social skills.

Children in this study had more stable friendships than was expected for such young children. The stability of mutual friendships from the toddler into the preschool periods of development appears related to the particular population of children sampled in this research. The toddlers in this study were not dependent on their parents for providing experiences with peers. Instead, they spent long hours every day engaging in intimate activities, including sleeping and eating with agemates. Some of these agemates appear to have become intimate friends. Exploration of the emotional function of early friendships for child care children, examining the parameters of friendship selection, and examining relationships within the child's family that facilitate the formation of friendships constitute exciting areas for future research.

CONCLUSIONS

Constructs representing social competence within each developmental period emerged in the predicted sequence. Children engaged in structurally complex peer interaction (complementary and reciprocal play) in the early toddler period and communicated meaning within peer interaction (social pretend play) in the late toddler period. Individual differences in these measures of social competence with peers were associated with individual differences in teacher ratings of social competence with peers and with ease of entry into play groups. Individual differences in social competence across developmental periods were stable. Competent toddler behavior with peers predicted preschool social competence as measured by sociometric status and teacher ratings. As predicted, individual differences in social experiences with peers were associated with individual differences in social competence with peers.

The findings also supported hypotheses that considered children's mutual friendships. Children in the current study formed stable friendships in the toddler period. Some of the friendships remained stable throughout preschool. Mutual friendships both mark social competence with peers and appear to facilitate the development of competent interaction with peers.

REFERENCES

Asher, S. R., & Dodge, K. A. (1986). Identifying children who are rejected by their peers. *Developmental Psychology, 22,* 444–449.

Asher, S. R., Markell, R. A., & Hymel, S. (1981). Identifying children at risk in peer relations. *Child Development, 52,* 1239–1245.

Asher, S. R., Singleton, L. C., Tinsley, B. R., & Hymel, S. (1979). A reliable sociometric measure for preschool children. *Developmental Psychology, 15,* 443–444.

Baumrind, D. (1968). *Manual for the preschool behavior Q sort.* Berkeley: University of California, Institute of Human Development.

Belsky, J. (in press). The "effects" of infant day care reconsidered. *Early Childhood Research Quarterly.*

Brenner, J., & Mueller, E. (1982). Shared meaning in boy toddlers' peer relations. *Child Development, 53,* 380–391.

Bronson, W. C. (1981). Toddlers' behavior with agemates. *Monographs on Infancy.*

Bronson, W. C. (1985). Growth in the organization of behavior over the second year of life. *Developmental Psychology, 21,* 108–117.

Brownell, C. A. (1986). Convergent developments: Cognitive-developmental correlates of growth in infant/toddler peer skills. *Child Development, 57,* 275–286.

Clarke-Stewart, K. A. (1983). Day care: A new context for research and development. In M. Perlmutter (Ed.), *Minnesota symposium in child psychology* (Vol. **16,** pp. 61–100). Hillsdale, NJ: Erlbaum.

Coie, J. D., & Dodge, K. A. (1983). Continuities and changes in children's social status: A five year longitudinal study. *Merrill-Palmer Quarterly, 29,* 261–282.

Coie, J. D., & Kupersmidt, J. B. (1983). A behavioral analysis of emerging social status in boys' groups. *Child Development, 54,* 1400–1416.

Connolly, J. A., & Doyle, A. B. (1984). Relation of social fantasy play to social competence in preschoolers. *Developmental Psychology, 20,* 797–806.

Corsaro, W. A. (1981). Friendship in the nursery school. In S. R. Asher & J. Gottman (Eds.), *The development of children's friendships* (pp. 207–241). New York: Cambridge University Press.

Dodge, K. A. (1983). Behavioral antecedents of peer social status. *Child Development, 54,* 1386–1399.

Dodge, K. A., Schlundt, D. C., Schocken, I., & Delugach, J. D. (1983). Social competence and children's sociometric status: The role of peer group entry strategies. *Merrill-Palmer Quarterly, 29,* 309–337.

Doyle, A. B., Connolly, J. A., & Rivest, L. (1980). The effect of playmate familiarity on the social interactions of young children. *Child Development, 51,* 217–223.

Eckerman, C. O., & Stein, M. R. (1982). The toddler's emerging interactive skills. In K.

Rubin & H. Ross (Eds.), *Peer relationships and social skills in childhood* (pp. 41–72). New York: Springer.

Eckerman, C. O., Whatley, J., & Kutz, S. (1975). Growth of social play with peers during the second year of life. *Developmental Psychology,* **11,** 42–49.

Espinosa, M. P., & Howes, C. (1984). *Social correlates of daycare toddlers' peer competency.* Unpublished manuscript, University of California, Los Angeles, Department of Education.

Field, T. M. (1984). Separation stress of young children transferring to new schools. *Developmental Psychology,* **20,** 786–792.

Foot, H. C., Chapman, A., & Smith, J. (1980). Patterns of interaction in children's friendships. In H. C. Foot, A. Chapman, & J. Smith (Eds.), *Friendship and social relations in young children* (pp. 267–293). New York: Wiley.

French, D. C. (in press). Children's social interactions with older, younger, and same-age peers. *Journal of Social and Personal Relationships.*

Freud, A., & Dann, S. (1951). An experiment in group upbringing. *Psychoanalytic Study of the Child,* **8,** 127–168.

Furman, W. C., & Bierman, K. (1983). Developmental changes in young children's conceptions of friendships. *Child Development,* **54,** 549–556.

Garvey, C. J. (1977). *Play.* Cambridge, Mass.: Harvard University Press.

Goldman, B., & Ross, H. (1978). Social skills in action: Analysis of early peer games. In J. Glick & K. A. Clarke-Stewart (Eds.), *The development of social understanding* (pp. 177–212). New York: Gardner.

Gottman, J. M. (1983). How children become friends. *Monographs of the Society for Research in Child Development,* **48**(2, Serial No. 201).

Greenwood, C., Walker, H., Todd, N., & Hops, H. (1979). Selecting a cost effective screening measure for the assessment of preschool social withdrawal. *Journal of Applied Behavior Analysis,* **12,** 639–652.

Hartup, W. W. (1975). The origins of friendship. In M. Lewis & L. Rosenblum (Eds.), *Friendship and peer relations* (pp. 1–20). New York: Wiley.

Hartup, W. W. (1983). Peer relations. In E. M. Hetherington (Ed.), P. H. Mussen (Series Ed.), *Handbook of child psychology: Vol. 4. Socialization, personality, and social development* (pp. 103–196). New York: Wiley.

Hay, D. F. (1985). Learning to form relationships in infancy: Parallel attainments with parents and peers. *Developmental Review,* **5,** 122–161.

Hinde, R. A., Titmus, G., Easton, J., & Tamplin, A. (1985). Incidence of friendship and behavior towards strong associates vs. nonassociates in preschools. *Child Development,* **55,** 234–245.

Hollenbeck, A. (1978). Problems of reliability in observational research. In G. P. Sackett (Ed.), *Observing behavior.* Baltimore: University Park Press.

Holmberg, M. C. (1980). The development of social exchange patterns from 12 to 42 months. *Child Development,* **51,** 448–456.

Howes, C. (1980). Peer play scale as an index of complexity of peer interaction. *Developmental Psychology,* **16,** 371–372.

Howes, C. (1983). Patterns of friendship. *Child Development,* **54,** 1041–1053.

Howes, C. (1985). Sharing fantasy: Social pretend play in toddlers. *Child Development,* **56,** 1253–1258.

Howes, C. (1987). Social competence with peers in young children: Developmental sequences. *Developmental Review,* **7,** 252–272.

Hymel, S. (1983). Preschool children's peer relations: Issues in sociometric assessment. *Merrill-Palmer Quarterly,* **29,** 237–260.

Jacobson, J., & Wille, D. (1986). The influence of attachment pattern on developmental changes in peer interaction for the toddler to preschool period. *Child Development,* **57,** 338–347.

Kirk, R. E. (1982). *Experimental design: Procedures for the behavioral sciences* (2d ed.). Monterey, CA: Brooks/Cole.

Ladd, G. W. (1983). Social networks of popular, average, and rejected children in school settings. *Merrill-Palmer Quarterly,* **29,** 283–308.

LaFreniere, P. J., & Sroufe, L. A. (1985). Profiles of peer competence in the preschool: Inter-relations between measures, influence of social ecology, and relation to attachment theory. *Developmental Psychology,* **21,** 56–69.

Lederberg, A. R., Rosenblatt, S., Vandell, D. L., & Chapin, S. (1987). Temporary and long term friendships in hearing and deaf preschoolers. *Merrill-Palmer Quarterly,* **33,** 515–534.

Li, A. (1985). Early rejected status and later social adjustment: A three year follow-up. *Journal of Abnormal Child Psychology,* **13,** 567–577.

Masters, J. C., & Furman, W. C. (1981). Popularity, individual friendship selection, and specific peer interaction among children. *Developmental Psychology,* **17,** 344–350.

Mueller, E., & Brenner, J. (1977). The origin of social skills and interaction among play group toddlers. *Child Development,* **48,** 854–861.

Mueller, E., & Lucas, T. (1975). A developmental analysis of peer interaction among toddlers. In M. Lewis & L. Rosenblum (Eds.), *Friendship and peer relations* (pp. 223–258). New York: Wiley.

Mueller, E., & Vandell, D. L. (1979). Infant-infant interaction. In J. Osofsky (Ed.), *Handbook of infant development* (pp. 591–622). New York: Wiley.

Newcomb, A. F., & Bukowski, W. M. (1983). Social impact and social preference as determinants of children's peer group status. *Developmental Psychology,* **19,** 856–867.

Parke, R. D., MacDonald, K. B., Beitel, A., & Bhanager, N. (1986). The role of the family in the development of peer relationships. In R. DeV. Peters & R. J. McMahan (Eds.), *Marriages and families.* New York: Brunner-Mazel.

Parker, J., & Asher, S. R. (in press). Predicting long term outcomes from peer rejection. *Psychological Bulletin.*

Peery, J. C. (1979). Popular, amiable, isolated, rejected: A reconceptualization of sociometric status in preschool children. *Child Development,* **50,** 1231–1234.

Pepler, D., Corter, C., & Abramovitch, R. (1982). Social relations among children: Comparison of sibling and peer interaction. In K. Rubin & H. Ross (Eds.), *Peer relationships and social skills in childhood* (pp. 209–227). New York: Springer.

Poteat, G. M., Ironsmith, M., & Bullock, J. (1986). The classification of preschool sociometric status. *Early Childhood Research Quarterly,* **1,** 349–360.

Putallaz, M. (1983). Predicting children's sociometric status from their behavior. *Child Development,* **54,** 1417–1426.

Putallaz, M., & Gottman, J. M. (1981). Social skills and group acceptance. In S. R. Asher & J. M. Gottman (Eds.), *The development of children's friendships.* Cambridge: Cambridge University Press.

Roopnarine, J., & Field, T. (1984). Play interactions of friends and acquaintances in nursery school. In T. Field, J. Roopnarine, & M. Segal (Eds.), *Friendships in normal and handicapped children.* Norwood, NJ: Ablex.

Rosenberg, D. (1985, April). *Fantasy play and socio-emotional development.* Paper presented at the biennial meeting of the Society for Research in Child Development, Toronto.

Ross, H. (1982). The establishment of social games amongst toddlers. *Developmental Psychology,* **18,** 509–518.

Ross, H., Lollois, S., & Elliott, C. (1982). Toddler peer communication. In K. Rubin & H.

Ross (Eds.), *Peer relationships and social skills in childhood* (pp. 31–65, 73–98). New York: Springer.

Rubenstein, J., & Howes, C. (1976). The effect of peers on toddler's interaction with mother and toys. *Child Development, 47,* 597–605.

Rubin, K. H. (1982). Social and social-cognitive developmental characteristics of young isolated, normal, and sociable children. In K. Rubin & H. Ross (Eds.), *Peer relationships and social skills in childhood* (pp. 163–181, 353–374). New York: Springer.

Rubin, K. H. (1985). Socially withdrawn children: An "at risk" population? In B. Schneider, K. Rubin, & J. Ledingham (Eds.), *Peer relationships and social skills in childhood: Vol. 2. Issues in assessment and training* (pp. 125–139). New York: Springer.

Rubin, K. H., & Clark, M. L. (1983). Preschool teachers' ratings of behavioral problems: Observational, sociometric, and social-cognitive correlates. *Journal of Abnormal Child Psychology, 11,* 273–286.

Rubin, K. H., & Daniels-Beirness, T. (1983). Concurrent and predictive correlates of sociometric status in kindergarten and grade one children. *Merrill-Palmer Quarterly, 29,* 337–352.

Rubin, K. H., Fein, G., & Vandenberg, B. (1983). Play. In E. M. Hetherington (Ed.), P. H. Mussen (Series Ed.), *Handbook of child psychology: Vol. 4. Socialization, personality, and social development* (pp. 693–774). New York: Wiley.

Rubin, K. H., Hymel, S., LeMare, L., & Rowden, L. (in press). Children experiencing social difficulties: Sociometric neglect reconsidered. *Canadian Journal of Behavioral Science.*

Rubin, K. H., & Lollis, S. (1988). Origins and consequences of social withdrawal. In J. Belsky & T. Nezworski (Eds.), *Clinical implications of attachment theory.* Hillsdale, NJ: Erlbaum.

Rubin, Z., & Sloman, J. (1984). How parents influence their children's friendships. In M. Lewis (Ed.), *Beyond the dyad* (pp. 223–250). New York: Plenum.

Selman, R. L., Jaquette, D., & Lavin, D. (1977). Interpersonal awareness in children. *American Journal of Orthopsychiatry, 47,* 264–274.

Small, M. (1976). Peer attachments. *Dissertation Abstracts International, 37,* 4707.

Sroufe, L. A. (1981). Forward. In W. C. Bronson (Ed.), *Toddlers' behaviors with agemates.* Norwood, NJ: Ablex.

Sroufe, L. A. (1983). Infant-caregiver attachment and patterns of adaptation in preschool. In M. Perlmutter (Ed.), *Minnesota symposium on child psychology* (Vol. **16**). Hillsdale, NJ: Erlbaum.

Tessier, O., & Boivin, M. (1985, April). *The coherence of sociometric nominations and the preschooler's understanding of friendship.* Paper presented at the biennial meeting of the Society for Research in Child Development, Toronto.

Vandell, D. V., & Mueller, E. (1980). Peer play and friendship during the first two years. In H. Foot, T. Chapman, & J. Smith (Eds.), *Friendship and childhood relationships.* London: Wiley.

ACKNOWLEDGMENTS

This project could not have been accomplished without the cooperation of the children, their parents, and teachers. Thanks to Laura Beizer Seidner, JoAnn Farver, Tagoush Der Kiureghian, Esther Braun, and Michael Espinosa, who worked as research assistants. I am very grateful to Deborah J. Stipek, JoAnn Krakow, Marvin Lee, Judith Golub, and Olivia Unger, who provided valuable comments on earlier drafts of the manuscript, and Judith Golub and Anthony Mischel for editorial assistance. Portions of this study were presented as part of a symposium entitled "Early Peer Relations: Ten Years of Research," chaired by Carol Eckerman and Edward Mueller at the 1985 meeting of the Society for Research in Child Development.

Correspondence and reprint requests should be addressed to Carollee Howes, Graduate School of Education, University of California, Los Angeles, California 90024.

TOWARD THE STUDY OF SOCIAL COMPETENCE, SOCIAL STATUS, AND SOCIAL RELATIONS

COMMENTARY BY KENNETH H. RUBIN AND HILDY S. ROSS

Every so often, an entire field of study reaches a point in its maturity that poses the question, What's next? So it is with the study of peer relationships and social skills in childhood. For the past 15 years, researchers have attempted to demonstrate that the peer group is a significant socialization force (Hartup, 1983) and that children who deviate from the norm in terms of their social skills or reputations among peers may be at risk for later psychological difficulties. In a recent review, Parker and Asher (1987) concluded that current empirical evidence leads to the safe conclusion that peer rejection and aggression in childhood are stable phenomena and that they are strong predictors of such negative outcomes as school dropout, crime and delinquency, and psychological disturbance in adolescence and adulthood. This conclusion has been supported by recently reported longitudinal data sets in which childhood aggression as well as childhood withdrawal and anxiety have predicted subsequent psychological difficulty (e.g., Rubin & Mills, in press).

Now that the writing is on the wall (or in our journals), members of our discipline might do well to take the information and run. Certainly, it is reasonable to ask, Run where? Some will doubtless begin to examine the ways in which peer rejection, aggression, and social withdrawal can be treated. Those who choose this route will find themselves in the company of active researchers and research-oriented practitioners (for reviews of the social skills training literatures, see Schneider, Rubin, & Ledingham, 1985). Others will explore the developmental origins of social competence and peer acceptance. Researchers who have begun this quest have tended to focus either on dispositional characteristics of infants (e.g., Kagan, Reznick,

& Snidman, 1987) or on early relationships within the family (e.g., Sroufe, 1983) as potential determinants of socially competent and incompetent behavior (for a review, see Rubin, LeMare, & Lollis, in press).

Howes's *Monograph* opens a third promising avenue for the prediction of peer social status and psychopathology in childhood. she demonstrates the significance of peer relationships in children as young as 12 months for later social status among agemates. But the *Monograph* is not limited to this finding alone. Howes also has examined and integrated a broad range of issues pertaining to the early development of peer relationships. Issues of the early development and changing character of social competence with peers, the development and stability of peer friendships, and the effects of peer experience and peer friendships on social competence are each addressed.

Data were collected in day-care settings over a 3-year period. Some 40 children remained in the sample for 3 years; their ages ranged from 16 to 33 months when first enrolled, and they were seen twice again at yearly intervals. A much larger sample of over 200 children was observed twice, first as 1–5-year-olds and then again 1 year later. Howes followed the children in both these longitudinal samples even as they moved between day-care centers. Nearly another hundred children were sampled once each to supplement a cross-sectional sample of over 300 children between 1 and 6 years of age. Moreover, Howes used a variety of techniques to gather information on the children. Each child was observed in his or her day-care classroom in the spring of the year for four separate 5-min periods. Observation began when the child attempted to engage in social interaction with a peer. Peer-group entry, complementary and reciprocal play, cooperative social pretend play, affect, and friendship (as defined by proximity and shared positive affect) were the focus of these observations. In addition, social participation status (active, withdrawn, average) was based on the observational data. Teachers rated the children's social functioning with peers, and three composite scores—difficult, hesistant, and sociable—were derived. Teachers also nominated three best friends for each child. Finally, those children who were over 3 years of age completed both a nomination and a rating-scale sociometric on their classmates. From these measures, the children's friendships, their friendship status (none, one, many friends), and their social status (popular, rejected, neglected, controversial, and average) were determined.

Thus, Howes has collected one of the largest, most extensive, most varied data sets to date on early peer relationships. In many ways, this study is a model for those who have advocated the use of multiple targeting strategies to identify socially competent and incompetent children. The sample is large, longitudinal observations are included, and the children are daily participants in stable, ongoing peer groups. Moreover, Howes fully exploits this data to ask a large number of central questions concerning peer social competence, social status, and social relations. This *Monograph* is full of precious findings; everyone will have his or her own favorite parts. Our own biases show as we recount what were, for us, the highlights of Howes's *Monograph*.

Friendship and Peer Familiarity

Friendship is a key construct for Howes, both in her prior work (e.g., Howes, 1983) and in this *Monograph*. Reciprocal friendships are defined in terms of mutual choices in the nomination sociometric. Incidentally, these agree well (72% of the time) with both teacher-identified and observationally identified friendships. It is the large sample that allows Howes to explore the function of friendship in her children. She was able to examine a subsample of children who were rejected by their peers but who had at least one mutual friend. Her analyses show that, for these children (but not for their more popular peers), entry into a group was greatly facilitated by the presence of a friend within the group. These children were also more likely to be rebuffed in their entry attempts with acquaintances, in comparison with average children; they did not differ from average in their rebuffed entry attempts into groups with friends. Thus, a child who is generally rejected by classmates gains entry into play groups by virtue of having friends within the group. These provocative findings leave us yearning to know more. Who were the friends of the rejected children? Given the data, is there any way of discovering why some rejected children had mutual friendships while others did not? What is it that differentiated these two groups? Did rejected children with friends have behavioral profiles that looked more like those of rejected children without friends or like those who were popular or average in sociometric status? Do the longitudinal data allow Howes to examine the effects of having a friend on social variables in the subsequent year? Answers to these questions might permit a more definitive evaluation of Howes's extremely important conjecture that friendships protect children from the typically negative effect of peer rejection.

A second innovative comparison facilitated by the large sample size relates to the social competence of children who remain in the same day-care class and those who move between day-care centers or day-care classrooms either with familiar peers or alone. The presence of familiar peers seems to foster some increases in social skill over time. Measures of complementary and reciprocal play and teacher ratings of sociability were higher for those who moved with peers than for those who ventured off into new classes on their own. One especially intriguing finding was that, in one of the samples, a large group of children changed centers together, and their social and complementary play exceeded even that of the children who remained together in the old day-care center. To quote Howes, "The presence of familiar peers in an otherwise strange setting may orient the children toward the peer group and focus their development of social skills" (p. 58). Children who moved together also had parents who valued their friendships, and this in itself may have enhanced the social competence of the children.

Predicting Individual Differences in Social Competence

The real meat and beauty of this *Monograph* is found in the extraordinary chapters on the stability and predictability of individual differences in social competence. Howes argues throughout that social competence with peers is age dependent; what is competent behavior at one age is replaced by newly developing competencies at the next. The identification of three markers of social competence is a particularly courageous act given our traditional avoidance of defining social competence at any age. The three defining constructs of social competence that are selected are (1) the ability to assume complementary and reciprocal roles within peer play in the early toddler period, (2) the communication of meaning within pretend play in the late toddler period, and (3) social knowledge of the peer group within the preschool period. Howes predicted and found that these critical markers of competence at one age period were strongly associated with the critical (and different) markers of competence at the following age period. These findings, then, set this particular data set apart from any other extant. They are interesting from a conceptual vantage point, and they most likely have some practical implications as well. For example, the toddler who is incapable of engaging in much complementary and reciprocal play could well be thought to be at risk for becoming unpopular. Given that peer rejection is itself a risk marker (Parker & Asher, 1987), the data take on added urgency.

The strength of this section, however, must be measured against its obvious omissions. While each of these constructs is defended in terms of the processes developing within each age period, it seems unlikely that a single marker at each age could adequately define as complex a construct as social interaction competence. Further questions arise concerning the measurement of each construct. Complementary and reciprocal play was defined as the proportion of social play with peers in which children exchanged turns and roles using different but related actions. Communication of meaning was limited to situations of social pretend. It was the proportion of all pretend play (social and nonsocial) in which children used complementary pretend roles. This seems to us a particularly limiting definition. Why should the communication of meaning be important only in the context of pretend play? It seems that communicative competence of any sort should be a marker of competence at this and at any other age. For example, the ability to produce comprehensible, nonegocentric utterances and the ability to gain compliance to one's requests should be an indication of communicative competence. Moreover, there are some researchers who believe that it is the ability to negotiate the rule and role structure around the boundaries of pretense, rather than the production of pretense itself, that is the more appropriate measure of social competence (e.g., Rubin, 1980).

⌈Finally, Howes makes it clear that the real marker of competence in the preschool period is social knowledge, and by this she means the ability to think evaluatively about the peer group⌋ Social knowledge of the peer group, however, was not directly measured; rather, it was assumed that sociometric ratings by peers would reflect the children's knowledge of the peer group. Although this definition may be appropriate, there is no mention of other potential social-cognitive markers of competence at the preschool period. Thus, a decade of work concerning preschool children's abilities to think about and manage their social environments is neglected (for a review, see Shantz, 1983). The bottom line is that Howes's choices of operational definitions are too restrictive and limiting. The reasons and implications of using proportions of social or of pretend play in the two toddler measures are not made clear; neither is the rationale for assuming that sociometric ratings by others reflect the social understanding of the child.

Despite our questions concerning the measurement of social competence, we cannot help but be impressed with the strong predictive relations found between the measures from age to age. Correlations in these key constructs range from .64 to .75 over a 1-year period—not bad in a science used to dealing with correlations in the .30s. In addition, the measures of social competence appear throughout the *Monograph* in predicted and explicable relations to other measures, thus greatly strengthening the nomological network. For example⌈children with more general peer experience and with more experience in their particular child-care group scored higher on these measures of social competence within the appropriate age periods than children who entered the peer group later. Children also appeared to be more socially competent if they remained in the same peer group as their friends from one year to the next. Each of these findings validates the measures of peer social competence⌋

Perhaps the strength of these constructs derives from their *not* being pure indices of the social competence of the individual child. Rather, each depends on cooperation or acceptance by other children in the social milieu. However skilled individual toddlers are, their social play cannot become complementary or reciprocal without a peer also joining them in such play; pretend play becomes cooperative social pretend only when another child cooperates in adopting and maintaining complementary play roles. Sociometric ratings are an even more obvious example of a measure that depends on acceptance by the peer group. Thus, each measure of social competence is put to the test of peer reaction and depends as much on that reaction as it does on the individual skills and abilities of the children. In one sense, this puts competent behavior to the test of its effectiveness. Children are competent only if their peers accept them as competent. This means that each measure of social skill is defined not only by the individual's competence but also by his or her ongoing social relations (see also Hinde, 1988). Consequently, observations of complementary and reciprocal behaviors and cooperative social pretense as well as sociometric ratings may be markers of competence at particular ages, but they probably do not "define" social competence, as Howes claims. Moreover, it is important to note that the stability of social competence was tested within stable groups and in the context of stable social relations. Since the social group contributes to the judgment of the social competence of individuals, the stability that Howes found from age to age must be understood not as the stability of individual differences in competence but as stability in the interaction of children within a stable social group.

Possible Conceptual and Methodological Problems

The longitudinal work on children's peer relationships has been guided primarily by the belief that negative markers in childhood (e.g., peer rejection, aggression, social withdrawal) will predict poor outcomes in adolescence and adulthood. Howes's work is a welcome departure from tradition in that her measurement appears to center on markers of the "good," not the "bad." This focus, however, has some unfortunate ramifications when Howes tries to link her measures of competence with constructs that have been defined in the past in terms of their negativity. One area where this problem of assuming that the lack of a "good thing" is equivalent to the presence of something "bad" concerns Howes's procedure for targeting socially withdrawn children. Howes indicated that she drew her methods from those of Rubin, who has examined the concurrent and predictive correlates of social withdrawal in childhood (Rubin et al., in press). Rubin has identified withdrawn children in his longitudinal sample in much the same way as others (e.g., Furman, Rahe, & Hartup, 1979), that is, based on observations of solitude. Howes varies from this procedure by identifying as withdrawn children who spend little time interacting with others in the 5 min subsequent to their having made a social overture. Thus, after observing a total of only four social overtures and following their sequelae over a period of 5 min, children are behaviorally identified as withdrawn, socially active, or average.

What are the problems with this procedure? First, it cannot be assumed that a lack of social interaction following a social initiation is akin to the consistent observation of withdrawal. A number of researchers have indicated that social initiations are rather infrequent for children identified as socially withdrawn or inhibited (Asendorpf, in press; Kagan et al., 1987). On the other hand, the social initiations of children identified as rejected or aggressive often result in failure and, as such, are followed by periods of isolation by the peer group (Coie & Kupersmidt, 1983; Dodge, 1983). Howes's failure to distinguish between children who refrain from making social contact to begin with and those who are isolated by peers after contact is made represents a serious difficulty in her work. Indeed, the behavioral profile that Howes provides for withdrawn children does not appear to differ from the profiles described in earlier work concerning peer rejection and aggression. Howes's withdrawn children have difficulty entering peer groups, display more negative affect (e.g., anger), and are rated as more difficult (not more hesitant) by their teachers than are their highly active agemates. These data suggest that what Howes is studying here may not be anxiously withdrawn children but rather behaviorally rejected (and perhaps aggressive) children.

In addition to the lack of observational data on social solitude, Howes does not differentiate positive and aggressive actions in any of her behavioral categories. The failure to consider the negative, then, creates needless ambiguities throughout her data.

A second difficulty concerns Howes's discussion of developmental sequences vis-à-vis the behavioral measures of social competence. Her predictions, and indeed her findings that confirm these predictions, are somewhat puzzling. Howes predicts that complementary and reciprocal play should increase between the early and the late toddler periods and between the late toddler and the early preschool periods; this prediction is confirmed in cross-sectional analyses. She further predicts that cooperative and reciprocal play should develop *within* the early toddler period and not show any developmental increments or decrements within either the late toddler or the preschool years. Longitudinal analyses also confirm this prediction. Taken as a whole, however, it is unclear how it is that preschoolers show more complementary and reciprocal play than older toddlers and why they are predicted to do so, especially when only the younger toddlers increase in this behavior. Similarly, development in cooperative social pretend play was found, as predicted, to be more evident in the late than the early toddler period; yet the preschoolers demonstrated the most social cooperative pretense when they should have been producing either the same amount or less of such behavior.

What Next?

What lies ahead for researchers interested in the development of social competence, social status, and social relations? According to Howes (Chap. IX), the origins of individual differences in toddlers' social skills derive from the quality of parent-infant attachment and socialization experiences. Clearly, the role that the family plays in the development of social competence, peer acceptance, and extrafamilial relationships requires further exploration. Sroufe (1983) and others have demonstrated that the quality of the mother-child attachment relationship predicts peer acceptance and both aggression and withdrawal in the preschool and early elementary school years. It would probably be of some value to examine the parental (maternal and paternal) socialization beliefs and strategies that predict individual differences in social development; surprisingly, there is little information concerning whether the development of social competence is a high priority for parents and what, specifically, parents of competent, aggressive, and withdrawn toddlers and preschoolers do to teach their children social skills.

It would be rather naive, however, to suggest that individual differences in social skills, relations, and status derive solely from early parent-child relationships and parental socialization beliefs and strategies. The interactions between infant/child dispositional characteristics and the aforementioned familial variables require careful attention (e.g., Belsky & Rovine, 1987). The roles of critical life events and social and ecological stressors as they interact with infant dispositional and familial relationships variables also require our attention. It would be nice and simple for us to tell parents that all they need to do to assure themselves of a socially competent child is to make certain that their youngsters are capable of complementary and reciprocal play in early toddlerhood and cooperative pretense in late toddlerhood. Unfortunately, life is complex, and so too must be the goals of researchers who set out to discover the "causes" of development. Howes has not shied away from asking complex questions, and, as a result, she has taken us several large steps closer to discovering the predictors of social competence, social status, and social relations in childhood.

References

Asendorpf, J. (in press). Beyond social withdrawal: Shyness, unsociability, and peer avoidance. *Human Development.*

Belsky, J., & Rovine, M. (1987). Temperament and attachment security in the Strange Situation: An empirical rapprochement. *Child Development, 58,* 787–795.

Coie, J. D., & Kupersmidt, J. B. (1983). A behavioral analysis of emerging social status in boys' groups. *Child Development, 54,* 1400–1416.

Dodge, K. A. (1983). Behavioral antecedents of peer status. *Child Development, 54,* 1386–1399.

Furman, W., Rahe, D. F., & Hartup, W. W. (1979). Rehabilitation of socially withdrawn preschool children through mixed-age and same-age socialization. *Child Development, 50,* 915–922.

Hartup, W. W. (1983). The peer system. In E. M. Hetherington (Ed.), P. H. Mussen (Series

Ed.), *Handbook of child psychology: Vol. 4. Socialization, personality, and social development* (pp. 103–196). New York: Wiley.

Hinde, R. (1988). *Individuals, relationships and culture.* New York: Cambridge University Press.

Howes, C. (1983). Patterns of friendship. *Child Development,* **54,** 1041–1053.

Kagan, J., Reznick, J. S., & Snidman, N. (1987). The physiology and psychology of behavioral inhibition in children. *Child Development,* **58,** 1459–1473.

Parker, J. G., & Asher, S. R. (1987). Peer acceptance and later personal adjustment. Are low-accepted children "at risk"? *Psychological Bulletin,* **102,** 357–389.

Rubin, K. H. (1980). Fantasy play: Its role in the development of social skills and social cognition. In K. H. Rubin (Ed.), *Children's play.* San Francisco: Jossey-Bass.

Rubin, K. H., LeMare, L., & Lollis, S. (in press). Social withdrawal in childhood: Developmental pathways to peer rejection. In S. R. Asher & J. D. Coie (Eds.), *Children's status in the peer group.* New York: Cambridge University Press.

Rubin, K. H., & Mills, R. S. L. (in press). The many faces of social isolation in childhood. *Journal of Consulting and Clinical Psychology.*

Schneider, B. H., Rubin, K. H., & Ledingham, J. (1985). *Children's peer relations: Issues in assessment and intervention.* New York: Springer.

Schantz, C. U. (1983). Social cognition. In J. H. Flavell & E. M. Markman (Eds.), P. H. Mussen (Series Ed.), *Handbook of child psychology: Vol 3. Cognitive development.* New York: Wiley.

Sroufe, L. A. (1983). Infant-caregiver attachment and patterns of adaptation in preschool. In M. Perlmutter (Ed.), *Minnesota symposium on child psychology* (Vol. **16**). Hillsdale, NJ: Erlbaum.

[**Kenneth H. Rubin** (Ph.D. 1971, Pennsylvania State University) is professor of psychology and Killam Research Fellow at the University of Waterloo. He is the coauthor (with Linda Rose-Krasnor) of "Social-Cognitive and Social Behavioral Perspectives on Problem-solving," in *The Minnesota Symposia on Child Psychology,* vol. 18, ed. M. Perlmutter (1986), and (with Greta Fein and Brian Vandenberg) of "Play," in *Socialization, Personality, and Social Development,* ed. E. M. Hetherington, vol. 4 of *Handbook of Child Psychology,* P. H. Mussen (1983). His current research interests are focused on the relations between familial and peer relationships and on the socialization of social skills in childhood.]

[**Hildy S. Ross** (Ph.D. 1972, University of North Carolina) is professor of psychology at the University of Waterloo. She is the coauthor (with J. Allan Cheyne and Susan Lollis) of "Defining and Studying Reciprocity in Young Children," in *Handbook of Personal Relationships,* ed. S. Duck (1988), and coeditor (with Kenneth H. Rubin) of *Peer Relationships and Social Skills in Childhood* (1982). Her current research interests are peer relationships in toddlers and the socialization of justice in peer and familiar interaction.]

YOUNG CHILDREN'S SOCIAL DEVELOPMENT: INDIVIDUAL
DIFFERENCES AND RELATIONSHIPS

COMMENTARY BY DORAN C. FRENCH

Researchers of early social relations have been predominantly concerned with understanding the sequence of early development and explor-
ing the connections among peer relations, parent-child interaction, temperament variables, and cognitive development. This literature has remained
relatively isolated from the large body of research concerned with peer
relations in older children, a literature that has been dominated in recent
years by the attempt to understand the nature and implications of individual
differences in social competence. Howes has bridged these areas of inquiry
by demonstrating that individual differences in toddler social competence
are predictive of individual differences in sociometric status during the
preschool period. She has thus established a previously unexplored link
between toddler peer interaction and later social competence. By utilizing
sociometric status as an outcome variable, she has grounded this work in the
large body of existing information regarding the characteristics of children
who are identified as socially incompetent by sociometric measures.

A major feature of Howes's work is her validation of age-appropriate
observational measures of social competence (i.e., complementary and reciprocal play during the early toddler period and social pretend play during
the later toddler period). She has demonstrated that these constructs can be
observed reliably, are related to concurrent measures of social competence,
and are predictive of later social competence. As such, she has made an
important methodological contribution to the investigation of social relations in young children.

Howes's explicit focus on the relationships of young children constitutes an additional strength of this work. Our knowledge of children's friendships is limited by the common procedure of investigating social behavior in groups of children who are only minimally acquainted or in laboratory investigations in which children have very brief interactional histories. Nevertheless, we are aware that even very young children develop strong emotional bonds with peers, that these relationships persist over time, and that children exhibit different behavior with friends than they do with acquaintances (Hartup, 1983). Howes makes an important distinction between sociometric status, which refers to general reputation, and friendships, which are bonds between specific children. She argues that friendships between toddlers are important and has proceeded to investigate this within stable peer groups over time.

In doing so, she has provided support for Hartup's (1986) contention that peer relationships are contexts in which important skills emerge. Howes argues that toddlers learn sequences of social behavior within the context of stable relationships. Findings that children who remained in stable peer groups and friendship relationships demonstrated greater social competence than those who left their peer groups or lost friends are consistent with this argument. Despite the attractiveness of these arguments, numerous alternative explanations for these findings exist. It will be necessary to utilize converging research methodologies (e.g., microanalysis of the interaction of friends and nonfriends, treatment studies, path analyses, etc.) to address this question satisfactorily.

Howes is less successful in her efforts to develop a sequential model of social competence during the toddler and preschool ages. Her definition of social periods requires elaboration. She argues that the organization of social competence changes from one period to the next but is invariant within a given period. This brings to mind a more classic stagelike model than can be supported here.

Howes's statements that particular behaviors or measures "represent" social competence at particular age periods are also unclear. If by this she means that these variables are measurable, associated with age-appropriate social competence, and predictive of later social competence, few arguments with this position are likely to be voiced. She implies, however, that these variables are central to social competence at these ages and that these constructs subsume other relevant variables. This can be questioned. Teacher ratings were correlated with other social competence variables at all ages. Could not these as easily "represent" social competence? Additionally, the child's failure to engage in coordinated play or social pretend play or to achieve high sociometric status may be explainable by the presence or absence of other behaviors (e.g., aggression, social initiation skills). Perhaps these variables will emerge as more directly related to social competence than the variables selected. The conceptual or empirical groundwork is not yet sufficient to justify claims regarding the relative importance of particular variables or classes of variables in the overall construct of social competence.

The continuation of the sequence into the preschool stage is also likely to raise debate. Howes argues that the central developmental process for the preschool child is the development of social knowledge of the peer group. Unfortunately, she presents no theoretical or empirical justification for this position. Her hypothesis is likely to be challenged. Gottman and Mettetal (1986) present an alternative model in which they argue that the central social task for the 3–7-year-old child is to achieve coordinated play, the highest level of which is fantasy play. It is not until middle childhood that salient social processes focus on the integration into the larger social group. The Gottman and Mettetal model thus differs from the developmental sequence presented by Howes in three respects: fantasy play is a central social process for a period longer than that suggested by Howes; integration into the larger peer group does not emerge as a central concern until middle childhood; and the focus is on integration into the group rather than on cognition about the group.

Instead of directly assessing children's knowledge of the peer group in the study, Howes utilized sociometric measures to represent social competence during the preschool period. She argues that sociometric measures indirectly assess knowledge of the peer group. Sociometric measures, however, provide information about the person being rated, not about the individual doing the rating. That raters must know the names of the classmates being rated provides only the most minimal assessment of knowledge of the peer group. Furthermore, because sociometric status is not a behavior, this measure is qualitatively different from the behaviors that are chosen to represent the other periods.

An additional limitation of Howes's work is the failure to assess aggression and aversive behavior adequately. The display of aversive behavior has consistently emerged as a major characteristic of children who experience difficulties with peer relationships (French & Waas, 1987). Individual differences in aggressive behavior with peers and noncompliance with adults are readily seen in very young children (Campbell & Cluss, 1982), and it appears that heightened display of aversive behavior in 2- and 3-year-old children is associated with later adjustment difficulties (Block & Block, 1980; Patterson, 1982). A careful assessment of individual differences in aggression would have enabled Howes to determine the extent to which this overlapped with her other measures of social competence as well as determine the relation between early aggression and preschool sociometric status.

The need to include measures of aggressive behavior in investigations of the characteristics of peer-rejected children has become increasingly pronounced because of findings of heterogeneity within the peer-rejected pop-